TEJASVI ADDAGADA

Data Management and Governance Services

Services

Simple and Effective Approaches

Contents

Preface

One early evening, I received a message, on LinkedIn, from a bank's vendor-relationship executive. The message was to check if I could assist the bank with sustaining their data management office. It is quite un-usual for me to receive a message with such urgency but I did leave a response the same day. The next day, while in a gym session, I received a call from the bank. "Is it an appropriate time to speak," said a coarse voice of a middle-aged man. I stopped my session abrupty, and we spoke extensively for about an hour on the challenges that the bank was facing in their data management and governance functions. The scenario goes like this - The bank commissioned an in-house office for data management with existing capabilities and skills. After an year has passed, not much progress and benefits have been shown to the leadership. To top the challenges, the regulators are pushing to remediate the operational issues that link to customer data. By reaching a certain state in the operations where things had begun to lag, the executive owner decided to float a Request For Proposal (RFP) to the consulting firms that could turn around the data management practices in around six months. How often do, I get to hear that? Not frequently, unless there are issues that are heavily weighing down the bank.

   ***

So, that's when I decided to write a book based on my experiences that would provide simple but effective approaches to setting up and running data management and governance services. There are firms out there in every industry that would have invested in their chief data offices but have yet to realize the benefits. This book is a genuine

i

effort to assist such firms to guide them in analyzing their existing data management strategy and then to analyze the gaps while leveraging existing capabilities and also improving them.

At the outset, an organization that is maturing, with respect to how it manages its data as an enterprise asset has to orchestrate continuous operational data management processes to actively manage its data. I have further simplified the approaches to implementing operating models that are based on the enabling culture of an organization. The operating model, when supported by services such as data quality promotion or metadata capture, provide optimum outcomes and benefits.

Someone once said, "It is better to get the town plan right before coming up with a route plan". On the contrary, many firms have their town plan without a route plan as their data landscape has grown inorganically. Re-discovering and standardizing the current data management and governance services or processes can overcome most challenges.

For ease of comprehension to business users, I have decided not to use technical details in what you're about to read, and I have used several challenges and experiences from my travels as examples. Every chapter starts with an overview of the engagement with the firms that have employed me for the data management and governance service implementation. Hope you all enjoy the book and derive pleasure and implementable insights from my writing!

Acknowledgement

I would like to acknowledge my family, friends and colleagues who have provided me with support and encouragement to finish the book. A special thanks goes to my wife Anvitha Addagada and our parents for their extended support during this period.

I would like to convey my regards to Mark McQueen from Future Data Consulting, and Pradeep Kumar for contributing exclusive content. A special thanks goes to Anirudh Bhattacharjee and Ramesh Dontha for their extensive and critical review.

Finally, I want to thank my good friend, Surya Jaipal Reddy, who agreed to sponsor the publication of the book. I also thank my Editor Barry Lyons for excellent and helpful edits suggested.

I

Strategy Analysis

A data management strategy defines the approach to apply existing or new capabilities in an organization to reach the organizational goals and divisional objectives. A strategy can be captured in a strategic roadmap, operational roadmap, product roadmap, business case or similar artifacts

1

FOCUS OF DATA MANAGEMENT, STEWARDSHIP, AND GOVERNANCE TODAY

"Can you come over to my cubicle"

"Yes, in a minute"

"Gosh! Do you see that the account statements for 10,000 customers went out wrong this month?"

"I thought we had everything taken care of with our new process. What went wrong exactly?"

"We took a hundred calls from customers this morning about a management fee that was deducted twice"

"That's strange. Let me dig deeper to find out what happened"

"Please do so and brief me on the course of correction that also con- tains an apology to customers. Let us also rule out the intervention of press and regulators"

After 15 minutes...

"Got anything?"

"I just received a brief from the "Quality Control" stating that there

were multiple reasons for the error. The management fee paid by customers through checks is still manually entered into the system. There was a delay in the personnel entering the details and the change in the date was not accounted along with a system lag in getting the fee accounted.

Further, based on a report the accounts of the customers were deducted as well."

"How about a workaround for these double deductions?"

"We cannot do reconciled statements today as the amounts are inconsistent between the financials, the fee and the accounting systems."

This was a conversation between the Debby Myers, the Chief Operating Officer (COO) and Sam Williams, the head of accounting. This was a conversation that happened on an eventful Monday morning, in their London Office. Sam had crossed arms as he sat in a chair, and tapped his legs on the floor with anxiety. Debby remained composed as she attempted to get a handle on the situation by getting multiple divisional representatives on the phone.

These scenarios are not only common in financial service firms but across all industries. The needs of firms particularly financial services require an increased need for regulatory preparedness as regulations around data quickly evolve. The business environment is undergoing constant transformational changes while the primary drivers for these evolving needs are advancements in technology and ways of operations. Data governance is now a new normal in most enterprises as demanded by regulations like BCBS 239, GDPR, EU No 1024/2013, EMIR, GDPR, and MiFID2.

Back to Origins

Most published books by leaders in the Data Management Industry state the context in which Data Management plays a key role in enabling business ownership of data. However, to understand the Data Management space better, we need to go back to the origins in order to understand its roots and, therefore, its history.

Data Management is the science of actively managing data definitions, quality, privacy, architecture and data life cycle along with the value and risk associated with data. It also entails the process of obtaining people, process, and technology capabilities to manage data actively across Enterprise.

Data Governance is an oversight on data management activities to ensure that policy and ownership of data is enforced in the organization. The emphasis is on formalizing the data management function along with the associated data ownership roles and responsibilities. In addition, governance also ensures that data management as a service is sustainable as a function thereby enabling active management of data.

Data Stewardship is an integral lever of governance; it can be managed as a separate function. Stewardship ensures active data management by engaging stewards who enable stakeholders to take on their formalized roles, responsibilities and accountability. It helps push data management through the grassroots of the firm to leadership.[1]

Data Risk Management is a practice of guaranteeing the effectiveness of data policy and operational controls of data in the form of people, process and technology controls. It is also defined as the practice of setting the risk appetite and acceptable tolerance levels while monitoring the strength of the controls.[2]

Chapter-3 will have in-depth details on the governance functional,

---

[1] Robert S. (2014). *Non-Invasive Data Governance: The path of least resistance and Greatest success*, NJ, USA:Technics publication

[2] Tejasvi A.(2016). *DAblog: Call it a success by integrating Risk Management into Data Governance*, India: Dattamza

organizational structure as well as discussion on alignment within an organization. A sample alignment of data management and governance in some organizations today is presented in Exhibit 1.1. However, a firm's needs and present organizational structure plays a key role in accommodating the formalized data management functions. No firm would boast about its data function. Nevertheless, a question remains

"How formalized and serious are they in actively managing data?"

1. In organizations with a modest maturity in managing data, the data management services tend to be run by the Information Technology department, but the governance function is usually setup and ope-rationalized by a Chief Operating Officer or Chief Data Officer.
2. Some firms unassumingly setup their data governance division and pass the ownership to business or operations. While data management dimensions are sponsored and managed by the executive owner of the governance function, the Chief Data Officer or data management office leverages the services of IT's function as required.
3. In less mature organizations, data management and governance can be owned and ope-rationalized by the IT department, which can pave a way for them to gradually move ownership to business and operations.

The goal of governance function is to formalize and enforce business ownership of data. As the practices in organizations mature, the above three models are experiences and situations that can exist in the same firm. As we get to the end of the book, you should be able to answer the question,

"Should data governance align with the Chief Information Office

or Chief Operating Office or the Chief Risk Office?"

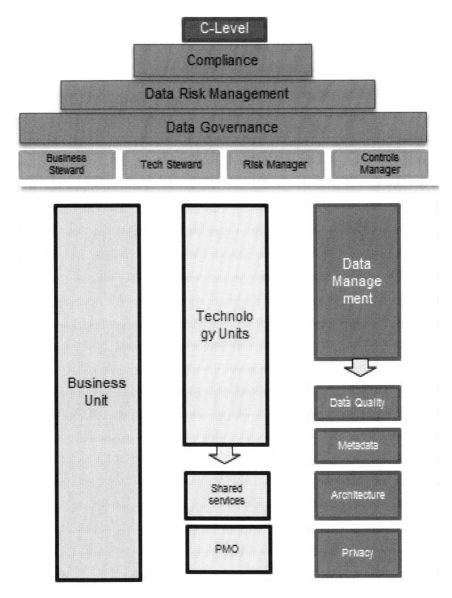

Exhibit 1.1 – Sample alignment of Data Management, Governance, Risk and Compliance functions

In the 1800s, horses were trained to pull carriages from London to Farringdon, which is to say that these trained horsemen were in the business of transferring people from place to place. This active process should be managed so that passengers reach their destination on time, a service that also includes the proper management and care of the horses. The outcome of this process is evident: the passenger reaches the desired destination, but the *benefit* of the service is that the rider reaches the destination on time and remains safe and secure upon arrival.

There also needs to be an oversight over all the horses, drivers, and carriages owned by the horsemen (or perhaps borrowed from a third party). Next, there is the need to manage the risks, which includes safety and security issues as well as missed timelines, all of which affects the profitability of the enterprise. Think of all the details involved that the company running the travel business is responsible for: establish guideposts all along the way to assess, monitor, and guide the drivers in scenarios of severe weather, faulty carriages, and alternate routes to take when inclement weather interferes with the standard route.

Likewise, with the analogy just described, governance is akin to evaluating, monitoring and directing all the aspects of data management: planning, acquiring capabilities, building the service, and then implementing and supporting the service or enterprise.

A common question that I often ask is

> *"Does your organization have a model that evaluates the benefits of Data governance?"*

Sometimes firms assume that "building value from data" is similar to "getting the right data fit for the purpose", though, the latter can be quoted as a necessity to get value from data. Data management professionals in the industry could, however, state the value from data governance, with ease, but in that case a change would be required in the perspective of viewing value from governance activities.

An Understanding of Benefits

A benefit is commonly described as

"an outcome of change that is seen as positive by a stakeholder".

Grasping the value from an outcome is, in fact, akin to making it objective and measurable. Oftentimes, coming up with outcomes like

"Making data fit for purpose" or "increased awareness"

is not-the-ask to mature data governance divisions.

How come we don't think of a cook you have employed as providing you with a service? The value of this service is just not to satisfy your hunger but also to provide you with rich nutrition, to deliver food on time, and to keep the risk of food poisoning at bay. Value is realized only when it is monitored and measured. In the above analogy, one can convert nutrition to a daily required limit (if, for example, caloric restriction is a concern); "poison free" is nothing more than a case of mitigating the risk that can be measured by the number of food poisoning incidents. Finally, counting the number of missed instances of having to serve plates on time is also another measure.

Focus of Data Governance Today

The lack of focus is vividly seen in data governance divisions and is always affecting how an organization pursues data management. There are immediate and cumulative benefits from data management and governance Dimensions, with either metadata management or data quality. Some data governance divisions kick-start their initiatives with the right business cases that overcome organizational challenges; these business cases should articulate clearly the tangible benefits of using these data services. What is it to the finance division, if the data accuracy improves to 98% from 60%? Does that mean that the financials that are made public need not be amended after they are published, thus avoiding compliance costs and reputation risk? This is feasible for firms that have known issues with Data.

But some organizations have challenges in trusting their data even if, their data is of sufficient quality. In such cases, benefits would be monitored and measured on a continuous basis following an assessment plan that captures the qualitative benefits as well. This can had from the use of industry maturity models and custom built maturity assessments.

Most organizations are not orchestrating data management activities as projects or programs but rather as a constant push- or pull-based services like data delivery or definition services. It is strongly recommended that the function has an assessment plan before starting a data governance service, be it data quality or metadata management.

This plan should bring out an approach that monitors and measures the value of orchestrating desired outcomes over specific time span. COBIT (Control Objectives for Information and Related Technologies) describes evaluation or assessment processes that place an emphasis on monitoring the performance of the controls from the perspective of both data management and governance (though governance processes place an emphasis on linking the assessment to benefits delivery). The COBIT 5 framework for the governance and management of enterprise IT is a business optimization and growth roadmap that leverages proven practices, global thought leadership and ground-breaking tools to inspire IT innovation and drive business success.

A sample framework as shown in Exhibit 1.2 presents governance and management in alignment with COBIT processes.[3]

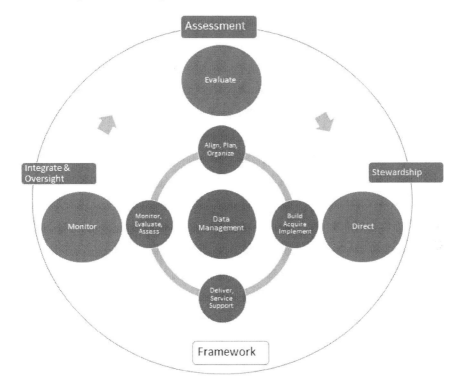

Exhibit 1.2: Data Governance and Management processes in alignment with COBIT

Think of every data management activity, such as data quality assessment, as an enabler, which, put simply, is a new or an improved capability made available to the organization to fulfill a part or need. These enablers can be further classified into business, process and technology enablers. For example, "policy-making" is a business enabler, "metadata service management" is a process enabler while "data profiling" is a technology enabler.

A common challenge that chief data officers face today is having

---

[3] *COBIT 5 Framework.* (2012). IL, USA: ISACA

these business divisions own the metrics that monitor the controls as well as the value from data management activities. While there are common enterprise benefits like reduced operational costs and risk, there are benefits that weigh in directly with the value chains of the divisions such as client service effectiveness.

Summary

Over the past decade, organizations have started to realize the importance of managing their data as an enterprise asset, though some organizations are far from embracing this data driven cultural change. With the advent of pervasive disruptors such as Internet of Things (IOT), machine learning, semantics and big data, organizations have started to realize that fit-for-purpose and trustworthy data is required to derive powerful insights for business growth. 33% of such firms are actively governing their data today, based on a recent survey. Most of these firms are also getting to directly align themselves to the corporate governance principles which is a two pronged benefit. There are immediate and cumulative benefits from actively managing and governing data. The focus of firms should be on differentiating data management from governance to achieve the data cultural transformation that includes people as major players. Further the focus is gradually shifting from having to mature data management capabilities to monetizing direct and indirect data benefits. It is strongly recommended that the data governance functions have an assessment plan before kick-starting standardized services be it data quality or metadata management. For organizations that do not have a problem with data quality, governing their data will bring trust in data to the people leveraging this data for decisions.

2

DISCOVERING CURRENT-STATE CONTROL ENVIRONMENT

It was a pleasant news that I was requested to travel to where most of the horses live, to perform a current state analysis of the enterprise. This makes it much easier, as co-location is one of major enabler in strategy analysis. The Chief Operating Officer (COO) always had a strong opinion on increasing the people's trust in data used for regular operations. The executive owner of data management, Robin, was based out of Rancho Cordova. Her statement always has been

> *"we do not have a data quality problem, but we have a problem with trusting data."*

Having the leaders, influencers, impacted stakeholders involved right from the strategic planning of data management and governance is required to build trust in data management and governance. While this can be achieved by a stakeholder management strategy and plan that addresses all these nuances. It also helped me immensely to understand the attitude of the stakeholders towards governance, their influence in actively governing data and the impact of these services on stakeholders at various levels. Based on the challenge, I was to put up an operating model after the organizational analysis in order to help the firm gain trust from the grassroots of the organization.

***

It was September, with the winter nights relatively dry when I took a flight from Hyderabad to Sacramento. I had to take a hop at Seattle with a stopover of eight hours where I enjoyed a good nap in the lounge. With a long flight of thirty eight hours, I wasn't particularly energetic, but thankfully I was excited. The climate was thankfully moderate, and the hotel boasted greenery all around.

As I landed in Sacramento, I did take a quick cab to my hotel where I put up for, close to two weeks. To my disappointment, my travel card was not punching into the "point of sale" machine in the lobby reception. Technology has advanced but it still brings up challenges! I could not get sim card as it was late in the night and I could have scooted to Walmart by hailing an Uber. But, I decided to check in, got to setup my wifi and Skyped the bank. I later got to understand that the block on the card, is an extra security feature enabled to stop cross-border fraud. Well, I always worked on (FCC) Financial Crime Compliance and could not complain.

Robin could not come to pick me up at the airport as her daughter was getting engaged the same day I traveled to Rancho. I helped myself with a good night's sleep to ease myself of the lag. I was startled to see her coming early morning, the next day, to pick me on her way, to the office. We had an early breakfast and to get rid of the Monday blues, we started discussing the approach to strategy analysis, over some sushi. I was intrigued by the sous chef's ownership of having to sculpt the fish to prepare my sushi plate. Later, I came to know from Robin that the restaurant showed standards in sourcing the catch, cooking rice, cooling it, adding vinegar, and maintaining it at the perfect temperature while he assembled the plate delicately. I was rather amused by the communication amongst the head chef, the sous-chef and the rest of the restaurant kitchen staff. This reminded me of the outcome that I was expecting from the data quality strategy. We further discussed our approach to strategy analysis over some fried calamari. The wasabi always had a burst of flavors ranging from sweet to spicy that tingled my taste buds. This got me thinking: Why not use a range of techniques from interviews, focus groups, and documentary analysis along with questionnaires to understand the current state of enterprise.

***

Challenges

1. The organization had a unique challenge with trusting its data or leveraging data produced by a different division or a third party.
2. There was never a data quality problem in the enterprise. But, there was a lack of structure where data ownership is aligned to business divisions while ownership still lies with technology division.
3. The knowledge workers had awareness of the context of data used by systems, processes and people but this knowledge existed in silos and was not documented to enable new capabilities.

Purpose

A data management strategy defines the approach to apply existing or new capabilities in an organization to achieve the organizational goals and divisional objectives. The capabilities can extend to people, process and Technology capabilities. To perform a strategy analysis there is more of business analysis activities than data analysis that must be performed to identify the needs of strategic or tactical importance. Strategy analysis focuses on defining the current state and leveraging the same to define the future and transition states. For a data management and governance strategy, the emphasis is equally spread across people and process capabilities contrary to the belief that it is only technology capabilities.

Strategy analysis provides context to defining and analyzing the requirements to setup data quality and metadata management services. A strategy can be captured in a strategic roadmap, operational roadmap, product roadmap, business case and similar artifacts.The Strategy Analysis for Data Management and Governance emphasizes defining the current, transition and future data management and governance states. The current state analysis covers strategic thinking in Data and Business Analysis as well as the discovery of solution scope to enable the organization to harness value.

If the outcome of cultural change is difficult to predict, the strategy needs to focus more on mitigating this risk, testing assumptions, and changing course until the capabilities that succeed in reaching the objectives can be identified. It was autumn and though the climate was as expected that day, it has not rained or snowed over the mountains during the previous two years. People were experiencing drought with occasional forest fires, a dearth of water in pools, and dried-up golf courses. What about preparedness for such scenarios?

I heard that even veteran firefighters have challenges predicting fire behavior. A range of techniques, from satellite mapping, weather information, remote sensing data collection, modeling, and communication, has changed the nuances of its behavior analysis. I understand the importance of quality data, and its operations, as it is used to save lives and reduce the threat to properties.

Likewise, it is crucial for firms to understand the holistic capabilities that could help them operate as per their needs. Is data quality being assessed for regulatory-related data while customer data, which is a priority for business enablement, not assessed? Today, a bank's customers, shareholders, and regulators call for a documented approach to data management that help them better understand the way to carry out data operations.

Current Organizational Structure and Culture

An organizational model defines the formal relationships and functional hierarchies among people working in the enterprise. While communication channels and existing relationships are not limited to the organizational model, they are highly influenced by it.

The values and beliefs shared across the people in the firm define the Corporate culture. These beliefs drive the actions performed by an organization. The opinions of individuals also decide whether guidelines or policy should drive the necessary behavior for data-related operations. Chapter 5 talks about these aspects in detail.

But, there is always need to perform a cultural assessment to:
1. Identify cultural changes apart from the required data capabilities.

- Stress the need to understand current people capabilities that include roles, responsibilities, and structure.

2. Identify whether stakeholders
   - Understand the rationale for the required future state,
   - Know the value delivered by the future state
   - Can identify the attitudes of stakeholders as they relate to the current needs and
   - Understand the existing capabilities and processes

The existing capabilities such as data querying along with maintenance of data dictionaries, describe how data management operates today to create "fit-for-purpose" data, though it should be pointed out that most of these data management processes exist in silos and need not be consistent across all divisions.

A capability centric view is required to know which existing capabilities can be leveraged to produce the desired outcome with fewer costs. A further capability-based view will assist in current analysis as existing features are organized in a functional hierarchy with relationships to other features, thereby making it easier to identify any gaps and inconsistencies.

Technology and Infrastructure

Information systems, applications, and platforms used by the data operations personnel need to be inventoried and analyzed as it helps in understanding system related processes, decision processes, and interactions with data suppliers and customers.

  IT divisions maintain the inventory of applications, platforms, their criticality to business operations, their role in reporting, transaction processing, and many more details, that can be analyzed through documentary analysis. The data flows, information maps further assist in knowing the coverage of data in detail across data landscape, data processing systems, processes across the life-cycle of data and the extracts and extract timings in distributing data.

Policies

Policies define the boundaries of the operation and guidance to decision-making in an organization. They, in fact, harness predictable behaviors for personnel through guidance, best practices, values and ethical ways of taking a decision that produces the desired outcome. Policy addresses routine operations rather than strategic changes. An analysis is required on the current policies that have an overlap with the current data governance program functions. This is to address any protection aspects that can be initiated by existing policies that have an overlap or duplication of outcomes between divisions.

Internal assets

There is a need to identify the organizational assets used in the current state of operations. The resources can be tangible or intangible, such as financial resources, patents, reputation, and brand names which need to be a part of the analysis. Further, the relationship among the assets along with the funding models needs to be analyzed.

External Influencers

There are external influences with the enterprise that do not usually participate in change. However, they might present constraints, dependencies, assumptions or drivers on the current state. The influencers are Industry Structure, Competitors, Customers, Suppliers, Political, Regulatory, Environment, Technology and Macroeconomic Factors.

Techniques

There are a plethora of techniques that one can use to come up with a current state strategy analysis. Business Analysts use most of these techniques detailed in this section. This book doesn't go into detail on the approach to these techniques, but information on using these techniques is widely available in business analysis and strategy analysis literature.[4]

Business Capability Analysis

This method is used to identify gaps and prioritize them about value, risk, gaps and maturity associated with each capability.

---

[4] *A Guide to the Business Analysis Body of Knowledge (Babok Guide).* (2015). IIBA

Business Model Canvas

This technique provides an understanding of the value proposition along with the success factors in delivering that value. It also helps when analyzing the total costs and direct and indirect revenue streams. It is also aids in understanding the context of a change and in identifying the challenges and opportunities that may have a significant impact.

Business Cases

This technique is more of an artifact or deliverable while it is also a technique used to capture information regarding the business needs, opportunities, costs and outcomes along with benefits.

Concept Modeling

This technique is used to capture key concepts in the business domain and to define the relationships between them.

Document Analysis

This technique focuses on the simple analysis of existing documentation on the current state, including documents created during the implementation of a solution, playbooks, manuals, vendor contractual agreements, industry benchmarks, trends, risk indicators and assessment metrics.

Financial Analysis

This technique is used to understand the effectiveness of the current state and the financial capability to deliver change. This assists in further understanding the strengths of the current funding model to implement data management across the firm.

Focus Groups

This technique focuses on having to understand the current state of the control environment. The group of nominated or selected stakeholders get together to vet-out or elicit the current state capabilities.

Functional Decomposition

This technique breaks down complex processes, systems, or relationships in the current state and aligns them with the organizational, functional structure that will assist in further understanding of the organization.

Interviews

A standard technique that facilitates open-ended or closed-ended questions to the stakeholders to better understand the gaps that still need to be answered after questionnaires, focus groups, and documentary analysis have been conducted and completed. This technique assists in understanding the current state and extended needs stemming from the current state.

Lessons Learned

This technique enables the documentation of failures, analysis, root causes, and opportunities for improvement in those programs.

Metrics and Key Performance Indicators (KPIs)

This technique assesses the performance of the current state of an enterprise. The metrics are used to assess the current state capabilities of the organization and will add up to the success factors.

Organizational Modeling

This technique describes the roles, responsibilities, and functional reporting structures that exist within the current state organization.

Process Analysis

The technique identifies the current state of the processes and activities in data management or other divisions. The processes might exist in silos across divisions and need not be consistent but can be or will be customized to their needs. If required the technique can be partnered with other techniques such as interviews and focus groups in discovering the existing process in case of non-existing documentation. While performing process analysis, the opportunities to improve the current state are usually gathered.

Process Modeling

This technique describes how a process works within the scope of the current environment. The models might exist as simple flow charts, process models in BPM 2.0 or ITIL or other custom standards defined by vendor solutions. If standards do not exist, the technique can be used to draft them in order to aid in future state analysis.

Risk Analysis and Management

This technique assists in putting the risks associated with the current capabilities to deliver their success factors. Further, any compensatory controls in place will be documented along with Key Risk Indicators.

Root Cause Analysis

This technique provides an understanding of the underlying causes of any data quality or compliance problems in the current state to further clarify a need.

Scope Modelling

The technique helps define the boundaries on the current state description of the capabilities.

Survey or Questionnaire

The technique assists in gaining an understanding of the current state from a vast, varied, or disparate group of stakeholders.

SWOT Analysis

This technique evaluates the strengths, weaknesses, opportunities, and threats to the current state enterprise.

Vendor Assessment

This technique determines whether all vendors are adequately meeting commitments as put forth in their data sourcing agreements like data quality thresholds, or if any changes are needed.

Workshops

This technique engages stakeholders in describing the current state and their needs collaboratively.

Finally, with the use of these techniques, I could capture the information that has helped me discover and document the current state of the data control environment. Next, I started using the heat map to classify the capabilities (organizational or divisional) based on their performance gaps and risks. The health and strength of the capabilities are required as this helps in planning for the future state through the transition state.

***

On Friday before I took a flight back to Hyderabad, Robin surprised me by planning a wine tour, as I had ended my day early in office. The weather was perfect for a wine tour; trees were shedding bright-orange leaves all around the buildings. It was a sunny and a dry day as we started. Our first stop was 10 miles into the countryside that overlooks the usually snow laden mountains. As we arrived at the vineyard, the place was crowded with an immense gathering of people around the tasting area. We decided to get ourselves out of there and drive further to an old vineyard that hosted a winery that dates to the 1800s. I remember watching the news back at my hotel, which was showing the pope's visit to States. And the vineyard that we were in, had its wine specially made for the traveling pope. There was a young lady in her late twenties dressed in delicate hues of blue, as she was to join someone on a date. Or, perhaps, it is to appeal to the visitors, to get to enjoy the tasting better, is what came to my mind.

Later, in the evening, I had dinner on the pier with Robin's family. The pier was wonderfully decorated, with private cruises and yachts in the bay. During the sunset, the seating area adorned in white cloth waving in the light wind, played with the vibrant colors of the sky. The restaurant adjoining the pier served us a soulful dinner; I particularly liked the minestrone and the Risotto that accompanied it. It was a perfect setting for someone to get married. As it happened, there was a wedding planned for that day. After an pleasant stay in California, I started back with my documentation of the current state analysis and the pleasure of having to meet guys from the firm.

***

Challenges at the End of Analysis

Based on the current state analysis, below are the problems that the firm was going through –

1. The customers and shareholders did not have a documented approach to data management that would help them understand how the data operations should be performed in line with the best practices.
2. Regulatory preparedness from regulations like MIFID II, require the focus to have quality data.
3. Lack of emphasis on the ownership and accountabilities for their data. Tackling shared ownership between business units.
4. Based on the culture, the guidelines are the best way to implement data management, but the guidelines do not clearly state responsibilities and accountabilities of data stakeholders.
5. The internal customers' reduced trust in data is leading to quality analysis in silos over the same redundant data across business units. This was leading to an increase in the operating costs.
6. There are no published processes for data quality monitoring, data definitions, and architectural decisions integrated into the projects and normal operations.

Benchmark the current state

After performing a current state analysis, a maturity model from the industry can be used to benchmark the internal capabilities of data management. Some of these models as shown in Table 2.1, come with their own set of questionnaires and aspects that are used to benchmark the organization. The emphasis of these models can vary based on:

1. Process and the nature of the outcomes
2. Adoption by people, Process and technology
3. Implementation of capabilities along with Risks and related

Benefits

4. Perceived data value from non-monetization and monetization of data
5. Data being traversed from being a transactional asset to an enterprise asset
6. Implementation of organizational structure, policy, lineage, metadata, funding and culture change

Always, organizations need not be comfortable with an industry model, but would commission the development of an internal maturity model that is customized to its long term goals. I have commissioned maturity models that in fact emphasize people, process and technology capabilities through sub-models.

Organization	Emphasis on	Level-1	Level-2	Level-3	Level-4	Level-5
CMM & CMMI	Proccesses that are characterized by applicability	Initial	Managed	Defined	Quantitatively Managed	Optimized
IBM	Proccesses that are characterized by applicability	Initial	Managed	Defined	Quantitatively Managed	Optimized
	Governed by	Reactive	Process existing for projects	Proactive and Process existing for firm	Process Measured	Process continuosly improved
Data Flux	People, Process and technology adoption, Risk and Reward	Undisciplined	Reactive	Proactive	Proactive	Governed
	Governed by	High Risk, No or Low Reward	Medium Risk and Reward			Low Risk and High Reward
Kalido	Percieved Data value, Data as an enterprise asset, Risk and Reward	Application centric	Enterprise Repository	Policy Centri	Policy Centric	Governed
	Governed by	Transactional asset, Data value not measured	Low data value, not much managed	Managed asset, Medium Value	Managed asset, Medium Value	Strategic Asset, High Value
EDM	Org Structure, Policy, Lineage, Metadata, Funding model	Conceptual	Developmental	Defined	Achieved	Enhanced
	Governed by	Issues Identified, Data people engaged	Project/Annual funding, stakeholders & policy identification	Active users, policy exists, Metadata, lineage defined	Policy Adhered, Metadata harmonized	Embedded into operations and culture

Table 2.1: Maturity models and their Emphasis

Summary

If someone states that we are directly moving on to defining the future state control environment for data, they are missing out on an important aspect of having to understand the current state of the organization's capabilities. Not having to analyze the organizational readiness to change, induces delays and redundancy in performing the current state analysis later on when implementing the new capabilities. While eliciting the current state capabilities, one can also get to uncover challenges from the stakeholders along with areas of improvement or extended needs in managing the data.

3

DEFINING TARGET STATE GOVERNANCE MODEL

After performing the current state analysis, I moved on to assessing the necessary conditions and capability improvements to meet the business needs. To add more context and diversity in experience, I am writing my understanding and best practices I have followed for other global firms with operations in more than sixty countries.

***

From the plush landscapes of the office in Bangalore, I was enjoying a mid-day mocha with my divisional head, in the Italian coffee shop, within the campus. They served good continental breakfast with baked beans which I particularly like. As a consultant, I am always on travel to the control centers of banks, and when I am not, I actively work with the financial practice to align our capabilities to the market while also helping clients who visit us. This stretch between engagements gives me time for my family and I to pull back a bit on the hustle and bustle.

As on the previous day, I got a briefing on the consulting engagement with a large bank, headquartered in the UK. The next day, I setup calls with the engagement management based out of London and Chennai. It was particularly difficult to perform a current state analysis, when not co-located, as it requires many endorsements from various partners at every stage of progress. These stakeholders included C-level and business unit heads along with application teams influenced or even affected by the onset of new data governance program.

Although there was not much I could do from Bangalore, I was particularly enjoying the leisure I got for myself. I had tied the knot to my fiancée, three months prior to getting this program engagement. One early morning in September, on landing in Heathrow, I took a cab to East Ham where I was to stay in a house share. I courteously declined to stay in a service apartment in London, as I wanted to experience the culture and make some friends outside of work. East Ham always had an old lingering essence of India, no different from a typical tropical city, with all its markets, temples, churches and electronics stores. There was no dearth of good Indian curry or breakfast, which includes high stores like Saravana Bhavan and, Taste of India while there were restaurants from other Asian countries as well. Then, there was West Ham which boasted some old taverns for a quick drink after day's hectic work along with a football club that helped me cool over the game and few drinks. I still remember having to walk early on weekends, to McDonald's to have my regular hash browns and pancakes while I could see the shopkeepers opening their shacks and placing their eye-catching electronics and toys in the display windows while people shopped the markets.

***

I Ubered myself to offices in Canary Wharf and Islington in London, for the initial weeks. I got the meetings and focus groups setup from various Subject Matter Experts (SMEs) representing Business Units, Business Analysts, and Architects from Data Management.

Challenges

1. The bank grew in-organically over the past few years through acquisitions and mergers that resulted in data redundancy from duplicated business processes.

2. Mortgage products, for instance, have distinct processes, leveraging the same data that is duplicated across the landscape while needing to maintain the products separately.

3. The costs were plummeting in maintaining redundant not-fit-for-purpose data and improving its quality.

4. At the same time, this was getting the attention of regulators and the customers due to interrupted services.

5. The unique challenges of a complex data landscape, commissioning redundant spends to maintain this landscape and redundant data and not able to leverage data to the rapidly evolving business models.

Purpose

The purpose of coming up with a current state analysis is to determine the necessary conditions to meet the business needs. These needs translate to data quality, content management and governance capabilities. It is required to ensure that the future state control environment is well defined, is achievable within the constraints and that key stakeholders have a shared consensus of vision on the outcome. Once the future state is defined, the existing people, process and technology capabilities including the organization structure will undergo a gap analysis. This is followed by an in-depth analysis of the gaps that will provide the desired outcomes. Some gaps might require new features, while others might require an incremental change over existing capabilities.

I was having a conversation with the program manager, and perhaps startled him by saying that

> "At the outset, a change may be needed to many components in the organization including Business processes, Functions, Lines of business, Organization structures, Staff competencies, Knowledge

and Skills training, Services, Governance Organization locations, Data and information, Application systems, Technology, and Infrastructure."

Business Objectives

I gathered the initial objectives from my interviews with the nominated stakeholders from the executive sponsor of data management and from the business unit stakeholders. The initial objectives are as below:

- Design and implement processes that manage and govern data for the benefit of all stakeholders leveraging it
- Benchmark maturity of the data management capabilities with external benchmarks and the needs of regulators
- Have clear, context-based definitions of critical data while having that data be fit for purpose
- Establish ownership and stewardship of data in business, in the grassroots of the organization
- Establish effective collaboration between business and technology stakeholders.
- Ensure that business units realize the benefits of managing their data.

Scope of Solution

The needs along with the new capabilities or capability improvements have been taken from interviews, focus groups, and questionnaires. These needs and capabilities were consolidated into a solution scope. The scope of the solution includes data quality, metadata, and governance capabilities. The following chapters detail these domains in depth. There are other dimensions like architecture, risk management that are outside the scope of this book.

Constraints

Constraints are the best way to showcase aspects of the current state and planned future states that may not be changed by the solution. A few constraints may include time restrictions, technology, infrastructure policies, privacy and security considerations.

There can be protection mechanisms from other policies that trigger a check on overlap with new data policies being published. An example of one such constraint can be protection against services to be set-up for data delivery in profiling the environment. The reason for this is that there are data delivery services that already exist for a different purpose. While a data management office can be business or IT owned, it is still bound to have this constraint. Some other constraints include:
- limits on the number of resources available
- restrictions based on the availability of skills
- a limit to the cost of acquiring capabilities

A skills analysis will be conducted to understand the skills needed for implementation. If there are constraints on re-skilling or up-skilling stakeholders, it must be well documented and closed.

An additional constraint is that certain stakeholders should not have to be affected by the implementation of the solution.

There can be constraints on ownership of activities and metrics for data quality by business units. Such constraints should also be captured, as it helps in the incremental and prioritized development of the solution capabilities, including the operating model.

Future State Organizational Structure and Culture

The formal and informal working relationships that exist within the enterprise can require a change, to facilitate the desired future state. A data steward can report to the data management Office today, but to enable business ownership of data through stewardship, the connection should be strong with the business unit. This might require a change to the reporting structure of data stewards. Changes to reporting and organizational structure can thus encourage teams to work more closely together and facilitate alignment to goals and objectives.

Putting an organizational model together required me to have extended interviews over iterations with data management stakeholders and business unit representatives which meant that I had to get onto early morning flights from London to Edinburgh. I preferred to travel from London City airport as it was just a 15-minute drive on early Monday mornings. Gogarburn was fun to travel to, with its vast plush landscapes in the campus. This was the time when winter was setting in, with occasional snow. I got a bit of flue as well but I reckon that the chef from my hotel offered me some pork and herb soup that did the magic and got me back on my feet. I had my room changed to a new one that boasted a balcony that opens to the river Leith. The place was once a village named Dean Village, northwest of the city center of Edinburgh, Scotland. The village once hosted a successful grain milling area for more than 800 years. The old buildings can be seen to be redeveloped and restored, converting workers' cottages, warehouses and mill buildings. Later, offered with a service apartment in the city center, I had much to explore with the queen's walk, the eateries around Christmas markets, and the national galleries. The sight of kids playing while enjoying the first snows, in the garden just opposite to where I was living was a sight to behold. On every Thursday, I flew to London offices for the next engagements with the distributed teams.

   ***

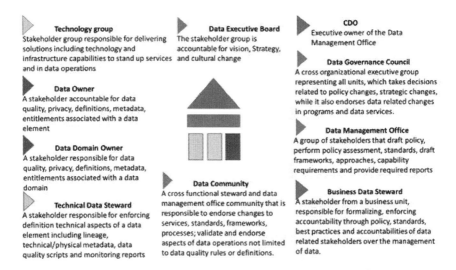

▷ **Technology group**
Stakeholder group responsible for delivering solutions including technology and infrastructure capabilities to stand up services and in data operations

▷ **Data Owner**
A stakeholder accountable for data quality, privacy, definitions, metadata, entitlements associated with a data element

▷ **Data Domain Owner**
A stakeholder responsible for data quality, privacy, definitions, metadata, entitlements associated with a data domain

▷ **Technical Data Steward**
A stakeholder responsible for enforcing definition technical aspects of a data element including lineage, technical/physical metadata, data quality scripts and monitoring reports

▷ **Data Executive Board**
The stakeholder group is accountable for vision, Strategy, and cultural change

▷ **Data Community**
A cross functional steward and data management office community that is responsible to endorse changes to services, standards, frameworks, processes; validate and endorse aspects of data operations not limited to data quality rules or definitions.

▷ **CDO**
Executive owner of the Data Management Office

▷ **Data Governance Council**
A cross organizational executive group representing all units, which takes decisions related to policy changes, strategic changes, while it also endorses data related changes in programs and data services.

▷ **Data Management Office**
A group of stakeholders that draft policy, perform policy assessment, standards, draft frameworks, approaches, capability requirements and provide required reports

▷ **Business Data Steward**
A stakeholder from a business unit, responsible for formalizing, enforcing accountability through policy, standards, best practices and accountabilities of data related stakeholders over the management of data.

Exhibit 3.1: A sample organizational structure with role descriptions

Roles, Responsibilities and Accountability

It is crucial for the success of a governance model to differentiate stakeholder responsibilities from accountabilities. Most of the chief data offices fail to have this clear distinction in the way they operate. For example, a data steward can be responsible for defining thresholds for data quality while the data owner can have the accountability to define thresholds and metrics. That said, stewards are accountable for ensuring that the data owners accept their accountabilities.

There are essential roles showcased in Exhibit 3.1, and responsibilities quoted in the Table 3.1 and Table 3.2 that clearly differentiate responsibilities from accountabilities. Most of the firms today fail in governance and stewardship due to the lack of differentiation between responsibility and accountability. Some organizations document the functional hierarchies to showcase the accountability. For example, in a scenario like data domain management, the data owners can be responsible for managing the definitions of the data-sets or concepts while the data domain owners are accountable for the same.

35

Roles	Responsibility
Chief Data Officer	✓ Is the executive owner of the Data Management Office ✓ Accountable for the policies, standards, frameworks drafted by DMO ✓ Responsible for the development and sustainability of the funding model for Data Governance and management services ✓ Accountable to the Project Management Office of Data Management Office ✓ Accountable reporting to Data Governance council and Data Executive Board
Data Management Office	✓ Responsible to draft policy and perform policy self-assessments ✓ Responsible to drat standards, frameworks and present them to the council for endorsements ✓ Accountable for the review, quality and applicability of standards of the Metadata in the enterprise data dictionaries and glossaries ✓ Responsible to ensure that SAAB CDM related data dictionaries and glossaries for critical data elements or enterprise data have golden copies, golden sources designated, published for metadata, data rules and privacy entitlements and classifications. ✓ Publish profiles and reports on data quality monitoring for critical data elements or enterprise data ✓ Provides auditable deliverables, assessment plans, audit schedules and audits ✓ Responsible to report on the policy self-assessments, escalations, quality reporting and other reporting requirements to the Governance council and executive board
Business Data Steward	✓ Responsible for enforcing accountabilities of data owners ✓ Responsible to ensure policy, standards are adhered to within the division/country/Demography ✓ Accountable for managing Data Quality, Metadata, Entitlements, Architecture, Privacy for non-enterprise data within the business unit ✓ Responsible for reporting on the data within the Business Unit (domains) to the data governance council ✓ Responsible to enforce policy, standards in the division/country related to Enterprise data/Critical Data elements
Technical Data Steward	✓ Responsible for data lineage, physical or technical metadata capture across organization ✓ Responsible to create data quality scripts from requirements/rules. ✓ Responsible to execute data quality rules against systems of records/golden sources, systems of reference/golden copies ✓ Certifies golden sources and golden copies ✓ Accountable for the management of data analysts ✓ Responsible to provide blueprints or architectural changes
Data Domain Owner	✓ Responsible for the definition of the domain and management of the definitions for data sets or concepts within the domain ✓ Responsible for suggesting data owners for the data within the domain ✓ Responsible for the overall reporting for non-enterprise data across all dimensions of data management

Table 3.1: Roles and Responsibilities in a governance organization model

Setting up cross functional councils

To have an organizational structure that supports future operational processes, certain activities need participation by a collective group of stakeholders. This primarily can include various functional levels and have representation from diverse divisions as well. One such stakeholder group can be a data stewardship council, which can have a permanent representation from data stewards of divisions and geographies along with the representation from the Chief Data Office and other stakeholders like data owners on invitation.

The council possibly can have the responsibilities of initiating any changes to the governance processes such as data domain, data set management or endorsing changes to the data quality profiles and metadata for business terms for critical data. Data in large organizations is not restricted to flow through one division while it can be leveraged by distribution across divisions. The stewardship council can invite participation from contributing and applying data owners to arrive at a common consensus on defining a data element. The group can leverage the breadth of representation over the organization to address some activities that cannot be done otherwise. They can in-fact be enabled and empowered to take decisions on frameworks and processes or to commission working groups for data quality or content management.

Purposing Working Groups

The stakeholder sub-groups are often referred to as working groups such as master data management or a BCBS working group. They can also be leveraged in setting up services such as data quality or leveraging existing data quality services for a program implementation like MIFID II. There are some working groups mentioned in Table-2, that are required to build the initial set of services and thus can be decommissioned based on the need.

Working Group	Composition	Responsibility
Data Governance	CDO Data Management Office Data Stewards	Create Vision, mission, plan Standardize dimensions to be pursued Draft Policy, review and get endorsement Publish approach and mechanism to policy self-assessment Establish Project Management Office Implement organizational structure Classify data logically into domains and concepts Create an approach to classify data elements into CDEs based on data management characteristics along with risk and value characteristics Create working groups for Metadata, Data Quality, Architecture, Stewardship, Privacy, maturity assessment, policy self-assessment, Tooling
Metadata Management	CDO Data Management Office Data Stewards Architects Content Analysts	Define standards and best practices for Business and Physical Metadata management Publish a Metamodel that includes attributes of Business and physical metadata Initiate a vendor analysis for tooling Define a SAAB Business Information Model (CDM). Crowdsource concepts and baseline them Standardize horizontal and vertical relationships across data modeling levels Define standards for capturing lineage

Table 3.2: Working groups and their Composition

Data Ownership

There has been a exponential growth and use of data by organizations in the past ten years. Industries in all spheres have moved away from implying that data is a by-product of a transaction to the realization that data is an enterprise asset.

This new view was partly fueled by data privacy principles which state that data that is Personally Identifiable Information (PII) must be processed under the accountability of a data controller, who must demonstrate controls for each operation as defined by the regulation that governs it. Thus, data ownership is the transfer of the accountability and legal rights on the creation, storage, distribution and decay of data to a single individual known as a data owner. The governance function defines data management policies that enforce a data control environment driven by data owners. The policy can enforce a simple rule as simple as not having to delete specific data from the system, for seven years. Another example of data storage control can be not having to store third-party data from a service provider unless paid for that use case. Capturing these data controls can be successful only with the data owners capturing this information and actively managing it.

Firms classify their critical data as Enterprise data, Critical data, High Value or Elevated risk data. The focus initially to identify data owners for the critical data. The organization states its in policies and beliefs that data is an enterprise asset but that it is employing data owners to take on the accountability of managing or liaising in order to manage its data.

Having the business stakeholders own their data is a crucial aspect of governing data. Having to differentiate the responsibilities of the data steward from the accountability of data owners is a stepping-stone in data ownership and accountability.

Data Ownership as put forth by many leaders in the industry is all about identifying, enabling and empowering the stakeholders to own the accountability and legal rights of data, preferably the ones who own the operational processes. There are many challenges in infusing ownership into an organization. Many regulators, including Prudential Regulatory Authority (PRA), have surveyed large firms and published the typical challenges faced by these organizations in pursuing data ownership. It's important to note that data ownership is usually not a full-time job for data owners whereas it is for business data stewards. I have given my advice below on gaining an advantage in the assignment of roles and responsibilities for data ownership, as follows:

- Accountable for conforming data to the policy, for the set of data owned by the data owner
- Responsible for partnering with business data stewards to operationalize processes that will enable defining data, it's metadata, data rules and controls.
- Responsible for reviewing privacy classifications applied to data and to stay abreast of changes when they are implemented
- Responsible for relaying news of a breach of policy to data stewards and the chief data office.
- Responsible for documenting data rules not limited to policy enforcement rules, data quality rules, transformation rules, notification rules and thresholds rules
- Escalate issues based on the notifications received from data quality exception report
- Accountable for drafting data agreements between data producers and data consumer
- Accountable for maintaining metadata, control requirements, classifications, thresholds, data rules, lineage and taxonomies for the data elements
- Responsible for publishing agreements with third-party data providers regarding usage, data quality, consolidation, integration and rationalization in advance of distribution of data
- Responsible for reviewing client- identifying categories and privacy classifications that are applied to data on a regular basis

***

Data Framework Gap: Who is Accountable?

Mark McQueen from Future Data Consulting states that historically, business leaders and executives have unfairly deferred to the technology function of their organization as the area that "manages our data for us" and, consequently, have not accepted their accountability for the data generated from their business processes. They have erroneously viewed data as an output of a technology process rather than an output of the business process that the technical environment supports. They have not wanted to be encumbered with data management activities because they see them as a distraction to their core business: selling a loan, treating a patient, or managing the finances or risk of the business.Data has continued as a technology responsibility even as the value of data is increasingly recognized as a critical component for managing the business, meeting regulatory requirements, and most importantly, as a key to innovation and delivering differentiation to customers. Early execution of a formal data management function for the organization has largely aligned with the technology function. Not to entirely let the technology executives off the hook, but many have been eager to keep the data accountability. In an environment where data is not governed, anyone who needed data would call their technology department to gain access to the data because as the keeper of the database, the authority to grant access to the data has defaulted to this department. By accepting the data accountability, they continued to give a hall pass to the business instead of demanding requirements for data. When the business does not define requirements for data as part of designing the solution, the result will always be inferior quality data—but this has been traditionally tagged as a failure of technology when instead it is a failure of the business process design. The business is the owner of the business process that produces the data and thus, must accept accountability to define and govern the data accordingly. This can fairly be referred to as the *What* side of the data framework. Essentially, the business must define what they want the data to do for them with business rules to ensure the data captured is appropriate for all its intended uses. Once the data is defined with requirements that are integrated into the business process, then technology can deliver the *How* side of the data: how to control the capture, storage, and transport of data through the data ecosystem. Only then will you have people, process, data, and technology aligned to capture and maintain high-quality data. "manages our data for us"

Black line Between the Business and Technology

Exhibit 3.2: Focus on Business Element and Data Element

As the owner of the business process that produces data, the business must not only be accountable for the data but also for the practice of data management. The responsibility to execute the data management processes, however, is a partnership with the technology department.

Within the data management practice, the Business executes the processes supporting the data *"What"*, and Technology executes the data *"How"*. Adopting the concept of a Business term as the *"What"*and Data Element as the *"How"*can help clarify this.

A business element is a unit of information that has a specific business meaning in the context of a business process or collection of processes within a business domain. It does not physically exist in the data ecosystem of a domain. Instead, it is a concept that when given structure through a comprehensive set of requirements, can be physically instantiated in the form of a data element, which is a specific unit of data that has precise meaning in context. The data element is the physical execution of the requirements of the business element with additional supporting technical controls to ensure data quality is achieved. This is the basis for the black line between the business and technology in an operating model. Stated simply, when executing data management processes the business is responsible for the business element and technology is responsible for the data element. The business is supposed to define the context in which the business term is created or used by providing description around the context. It is much better for the business to define what "customer" means as a business term. Management of the physical data model, along with the physical instantiation of the data element in the database, will be managed with the technology services. On the surface, this appears oversimplified, but all data management processes revolve around the business element and the data element.

***

Overcoming Ten Common Challenges in Data Ownership

1. A common challenge while identifying data owner is "Should this be a process owner or an application owner or a people (users') manager?" Data owners are often business analysts, process owners, application owners, project managers, SMEs, or knowledge workers. They can support processes, people, and applications that use specific data and they also have familiarity and knowledge of data in their scope. Usually, the firms that are kick-starting data management as a formalized function, tend to have the data ownership align with Information Technology (Application owners) while mature organizations have it with aligned with the COO or CDO organization. The stakeholders who have substantial knowledge of the business processes along with the data created or used by the processes will be apt for the role of a data owner.

2. To complement the technical know how—the data flows between systems, processes, and people—the role of the Subject Matter Expert (SME) or Co-Owner can be standardized.

3. Data owners have the responsibility for ensuring controls related to data are actively managed, and he or she can be complemented by an SME who has shared knowledge of the same data.

4. SME and Co-Owner roles should be standardized and consulted by stewards and data owners whenever required. The responsibilities of governing data should still lie with the data owner. Standardizing support roles through formal organizational structure assists in active management of data control environment.

5. There are potential benefits to having an ownership model that defines contributing and viewing data owners for data along its life cycle. For example, a contributing data owner is the owner of the data domain like customer domain in whose purview the Know-Your-Customer (KYC) data is created. There is the risk and compliance domain, which has shared ownership of the same

KYC data based on the context in which the customer data is being used in risk modeling. In this scenario, the risk and compliance function can be a viewer domain. It is beneficial to have one contributing data owner and multiple data viewers unless the same data element is being enriched and edited for context across various business processes.

6. Knowledge of data management and governance processes, techniques, tools are required by data owners to orchestrate data governance activities. These are familiar challenges that need to be addressed by up-skilling the data owners, which will enable them to take responsibility for managing the data actively. While formalization of the data management and governance activities is achieved through standardizing them as services, promotion of these services is still a major challenge.

7. If data owners have a business familiarity with the data but don't necessarily understand the flow of data along its value chain, it will be a challenge to leverage metadata management and data quality services. The data owners should have basic knowledge of leveraging lineage as documented in data flow diagrams or metadata repositories.

8. A culture of business ownership along with associated data governance services should be promoted in the Enterprise. This assists to builds awareness across the grassroots of the organization. Promotion of data quality, metadata, architecture, risk and privacy services should take significance on par with service usage and service improvement activities.

9. Data owners should be aware of the outcomes and benefits of leveraging data governance services. They can then assist other stakeholders in their sphere of influence to look for value beyond their regular line of sight.

10. Cascade the goals of an enterprise associated with data governance to the data owners so that the overall assessment plan takes their performance into account.

Capabilities and Processes

Defining an Operating Model

A well-defined operating model plays a vital role in achieving expected business benefits. Embarking on a data governance journey in an enterprise that spans divisions, geographies, and diverse stakeholders requires a good understanding of how various nuances of data management needs to be span and orchestrated. The essential aspects of a winning business operating model should encompass the following:

- Identification of responsible and accountable stakeholders
- Defining communication handshakes and artifact hand-offs
- Discovering and standardizing processes and procedures based on policies and guidelines
- Motivation, goals, and performance assessment to monitor progress and report on the quality of the data operations
- Change control with a well-planned stakeholder communication strategy
- Implementation of a road-map with a work breakdown structure

Customizing it to the culture

As I start to define an operating model in an organization, I explore the choices of centralized and decentralized models from the perspectives of the benefits and readiness in the organization. If a benefit arising from centralizing the data management operations across the enterprise is more than 20% compared to the decentralized model, the focus should be to centralize.

Below are some high level benefits that often go with a centralized model:

- The skills are not available in distributed functions while skills gaps are bridged with a central skilled function

- Processes yield consistent outcomes, irrespective of the business unit using the services
- Reporting is much easier to aggregate and present to leadership
- Decision making and executive buy in at the C-level is synonymous
- Continuous feedback elicitation, improvements and change in management can be planned for effectiveness.

On the flip side, friction in operations, reduced motivation in mid-level managers and bureaucracy at senior level often outweigh the benefits of a centralized model. That's where the socio-cultural aspects have a major say in developing the operating model. Attaining a fine equilibrium between assessing, directing and managing data is essential. This equilibrium also enables self-service in the longer run, though there might be a need for initial re-skilling of personnel in distributed teams.

A centralized operating model takes a top-down approach from leadership to grassroots while it emphasizes definition and implementation of policy. The costs and funding is controlled centrally by a function that evaluates, monitors, and directs the organization on data management practices. The stewards in this scenario will be from the senior level management and will be closely aligned with C-level.

A federated or decentralized, model on the other hand, emphasizes distributed management of data, with self-service as a major enabler. It uses a bottom-up approach to enable governance. In organizations where the mid-level management rather than the C-level is keener on managing data as an asset, the distributed model is suitable. The room for customization is enormous, while the management feels significant in its contribution to the organization. The mid-level managers in distributed divisions are empowered to setup their customized processes though a forum of such cross-functional management can be used to assess and monitor the service usage. The data stewards in this scenario will be from mid-level management and will be closer to the operational personnel of the organization.

A hybrid approach, as the name suggests, balances the direction and management of the data management and governance services. This is an ideal approach, when the C-level, along with the grassroot stakeholders, have the same level of interest in managing data as an enterprise asset. The control stays with a central function, such as the data management office which monitors and directs the services while the mid-level management has a major say in planning, managing and evaluating the services. This is a more mature variant of an operating model and creates a measurable impact on the organization. Each of the operating model variant's emphasis is showcased in Table 3.3.

Approach	Operating Model	Emphasis on
Top Down	Centralized	Policy, Guidelines, Costs
Bottom Up	Federated or Distributed	Self-Service, Management
Balanced or Hybrid Approach	Centralized Monitoring and Direction, Distributed Management	Needs, Impacts and Maturity

Table 3.3: Emphasis on approach to operating model

Each variant (e.g., centralization or decentralization or fusion) of data management operating model has its merits and demerits as showcased in Table 3.4.

48

Features	Centralized	Federated
Benefits management	Easy to manage & communicate to sponsors and data executive board	Can be managed well by business unit's data management committee if the unit is operating independently.
Ownership/ Accountability	Rules, profiles and results elicited and owned by a central cross-functional team. Only for "data at rest"	Rules, profiles, results elicited, owned by application owners & business units. For data "at rest" and "in motion"
Change management	Leadership intensive program Top down approach	Data stewards/data owners and application owners are change agents at grassroots
Turnaround time for orchestration	High	Low
Skills	Highly skilled team required	Regular skills with re-skilling will suffice
Personnel and process Efficiency	Central team's efficiency will be high, Process efficiency is high	Teams' efficiency depends on localized skills
Process maintenance	Easy to maintain	Often ignored
Stakeholder handshakes and handoffs	High in number and documentation	Less in number and based on LoB standards
Establishing cross dimension levers (metadata management)	Nimble to address in framework	Not simple to address
Continuous feedback elicitation	Planned and time intensive to attain from knowledge workers	Easy to elicit in silos, but often reactive
Rules elicitation & management	Dependent on SMEs, Highly Systematic	Localized knowledge exists, Less systematic
Framework View and maintenance	Centralized view and continuous improvement possible	Siloed view, improvements often neglected
Service monitoring, reporting	Easy at enterprise level	Cumbersome at enterprise level
Prioritizing DQ issues	Effort intensive	Less intensive
Tool access & management	Lies with central team, Vendor relationship easy to maintain	Dependent on the governance and quality tool owner
Data sourcing	Easy if using a centralized datamart for profiling	Easy if using the application data store but not central mart
Knowledge management	Driven by global communication strategy	Driven locally and depends on effective local management
Attitude towards data quality	Positive as orchestrated by central team	Less positive across distributed teams, can face resistance in pockets
Group policy implications	Easy to analyze impact	Difficult to analyze impact
Infrastructure	Central control over infrastructure	Decentralized control if using distributed data systems
Service improvements	Easy to elicit, change and push for subscription	Less systematic and application agnostic

Table 3.4: Centralized vs Federated features

On completing the current state analysis of the firm and its culture, one can use the outcomes from this section to customize an operating model. It is always suggested to have an operating model that provides centralized control and an approach to distributed management, as showcased in Exhibit. As stated earlier in this section, it can be achieved by balancing the responsibility and accountability of data ownership and stewardship in the chief data office and divisional data operations.

Data Management processes

The next step is to define the processes from a high to low level of details. I usually prefer doing this in BPMN in Visio, but the stakeholders in the chief data office along with stewards might prefer a different representation like ITIL. The outcome of the available current state analysis, where current state processes have been documented can be leveraged at this stage. There are tools from IBM like Blueworks that enable discovery of goals, milestones, processes, and Key Performance Indicators (KPIs). Such tools enable collaboration while also discovering the processes and simulating them. Some high-level processes along with activities are available in Table 3.5.

There is a difference in processes that are used to setup governance functions, while there are processes that are used for daily data management operations like data quality monitoring. The earlier is defined for planning from an implementation roadmap and also for getting a buy-in from the leadership while the later operational processes are maintained regularly. The details of the stakeholders responsible for these strategic activities mentioned in Table 3.5 are not presented so as to leave them to the discretion of the chief data office.

High Level process	Process	Activities
Define, operationalize data governance	Data governance structure is created	Commission Data Governance Office
		Assign ownership and privileges to an executive Owner (CDO)
		Create a Data Governance plan
		Establish and integrate with Project Management office (PMO)
		Implement organization structure, assign and enable roles
	Content Governance is defined	Define and publish Data domains, datasets or concepts
		Establish criteria to define critical data elements
		Establish alignment with Metadata Management
		Establish Data classifications including Data management characteristics (aka Master, reference), Data security and privacy
		Define taxonomies and ontologies
	Policy and standards are drafted and approved	Draft data management and governance policy and standards
		Review and endorse Policy and standards
		Establish approach and mechanism to policy self-assessment

Table 3.5: High level Data Governance

As the data governance processes are defined, the need is to define the data management processes and integrate them with the governance processes. The data management processes at various levels are available in Table 3.6–3.10. The owners of the data management can be the technology office, while the owner of the governance function can be business or operations. Irrespective of having a single owner or dual owners for both the functions, it is a best practice to standardize the process with stakeholders from both the functions.

Data Management processes	Data Management level-1 processes	Data Management level-2 processes
Define, communicate and endorse Data Management Strategy	Define, communicate and endorse Data Management Strategy	Develop Data Management Strategy
		Check alignment with Organizational objectives
		Define approval mechanism
		Evaluate and publish goals and strategy
	Elicit, prioritize, communicate and package high level Business requirements	Capture, define, analyze, prioritize, package and communicate High level business requirements
		Get sign off on Requirements from relevant stakeholders using the mechanism in the strategy
	Define the importance of identifying, prioritizing and appropriate use of authorized data domains	Define needs to identify logical classification of Data landscapes
		Articulate the importance of establishing policy to enforce appropriate use of authorized data domains, datasets and concepts in an information model.
	Define the importance of establishing risk management, integrating it with Data Management	Define the need to have alignment with Risk Management
		Align Data Risk Management objectives with Data Management Strategy
		Describe Target structure and organizational structure of Data Risk Management
		Define data risk management policy
		Define implementation roadmap and capabilities
	Align with architectural, IT and operational capabilities	Incorporate Data architecture concepts
		Incorporate Technology concept
		Incorporate Operational concepts
	Define how the data management program will be measured and evaluated.	Define the importance of developing outcome metrics to determine the effectiveness of the data management program
		Define the importance of developing tracking and adherence metrics to determine how the data management program itself will be measured.
	Create stakeholder communication strategy	Set the need to establishing a communication strategy
		Emphasize the need for up-skill and re-skill programs to identified stakeholders
		Define a stakeholder communication strategy
Define Business case and sustainable funding model	Define and Publish data management business case and align it to strategic value and risk drivers and tangible business outcomes.	Align Data Management Business Case with drivers, objectives and strategy
		Define business outcomes at a high level, qualitative and quantitative
		Communicate and Publish Business case

Table 3.6: Data Management Strategy and Business case

Data Management processes	Data Management level-1 processes	Data Management level-2 processes
Define and operationalize Data Management program	Establish and Enable data management program	Define charter for data management program
		Communicate data management program and provide rights of enforcement for compliance
	Develop, socialize and Approve strategic, operational roadmaps and program plans.	Develop Program plans in alignment with strategic and operational roadmaps
		Communicate Program plans and get them endorsed by responsible stakeholders
		Break down into projects and Create Project plans by detailing deliverables, timelines and milestones
	Operationalize Stakeholder engagement	Nominate stakeholders including sponsors, project stakeholders and define responsibilities accountabilities
		Funds are allocated and aligned to programs and working groups
	Define and apply stakeholder management and Communication plan	Define communication plans based on strategy, create channel of communication and publish the same
		Define Communication plans with external regulators bodies and get them endorsed
		Engage with internal stakeholders, external industry and regulatory bodies as per plan
	Evaluate operational Data Management activities	Establish mechanism to assess progress of activities
		Define and operationalize Issue identification, prioritization, escalation and conflict resolution
		Define and monitor Metrics (i.e.: KPIs, KRIs) to track Program progress

Table 3.7: Define and Ope-rationalize Data Management Program

The benefits based view of the implementing data architectural processes are:

1. Reduces time spent on eliciting future state architectural, integration requirements
2. Reduce stakeholder communication overhead with common understanding of the landscape, systems, processes and how data is created and used
3. Provides specific standards that imparts confidence in data
4. provides ease of sharing inter-operable data across services, systems, applications with less effort
5. Increased productivity gains related to increased availability of data
6. Reduced upfront costs such as maintenance of legacy systems,

transformations, and decommissioning of information systems

7. Reduced future costs associated with maintaining duplicated information

8. Increase in efficiency of implementation of other dimensions including Metadata and data lifecycle

Data Management processes	Data Management level-1 processes	Data Management level-2 processes
Define Technology Architecture strategy and service	Define and Implement Technology architecture	Define, communicate and endorse Technology architecture strategy
		In case of architectural solutions, or capabilities that include data quality or metadata, develop and align with the strategic roadmap
		Define and operationalize Platform governance structure and processes
	Identify and Govern Data technology tool stack	Define the Technology tool stack for selection of solution capabilities
		Technology tool roadmap is developed and implemented
		Tool selection governance structure and processes are operational
	Define and Govern data storage (lifecycle) management strategy	Define the Data storage management strategy
		Develop and implement Data storage management roadmap
		Operationalize storage governance structure and processes
	Implement Operational Data risk planning	Data service and infrastructure risk management policy, practices are defined and operational
		Define a risk register along with inherent risks, conduct Risk Control self-assessments, define residual risks and endorse action plans
		Operational Risk Governance Structure and processes are in place and operational through projects and in prioritized data operations

Table 3.8: Architecture Strategy and services

The benefits based view of the Metadata management processes are:

1. Increase in availability of information associated with data elements that helps in actively assessing quality, governing on a regular basis.

2. Reduced turnaround time to find answers during analysis

3. Increased efficiency of Subject Matter Experts in turning out information for impact analysis

4. Simplification of the data landscape by discovering logical classi-

fications and discovering redundancies

5. Provides consistency of definitions that assists in standardization of business terms and the context in which they are leveraged

6. Removes ambiguity in relationships among data in the landscape

Data Management processes	Data Management level-1 processes	Data Management level-2 processes
Metadata Management	Classify data logically and physically based on Business alignment and data management characteristics	Identify, document, endorse and communicate logical domains of data
		Identify, document and inventory underlying physical repositories of data
		Classify physical domains of data into Master, Reference and Transaction
	Define the data (semantically and structurally)	Document data definitions and associated Business, Operational and Technical metadata
		Establish vertical lineage between various levels of data - Semantic/Conceptual/Logical/Physical
		Establish relationships across horizontal levels including synonyms, alternate names, specifies, and generalizes.
		Document Lineage associated with data elements
		Create, capture, maintain and Govern Taxonomies and ontologies.
	Govern the data (establish sustainable data architecture governance)	Establish Data architecture governance procedures to control changes to the landscape
		Operationalize Data architecture governance procedures and align with Business and technology functions

Table 3.9: Metadata Management

The benefits based view of the Data Quality capabilities are:

1. Reduces operational costs due to reduction in number of data quality issues in data used by new capabilities, projects, reports and analytical models

2. Enhances efficiency of analytical models

3. Imparts confidence in data and supports quality assurance

4. Reduces general and administrative costs such as cost of IT personnel, business and technical support

5. Increases productivity gain of the personnel leveraging the quality data

6. Reduced up front costs, such as acquisition costs, integration and

training costs

7. Reduced future costs, such as maintenance, migration, and decommissioning information systems

Data Management processes	Data Management level-1 processes	Data Management level-2 processes
Define and operationalize Data Quality Service	Establish Data quality program	Define, communicate and endorse data quality strategy, target state objectives and approach
		Identify accountable parties along with roles and responsibilities
		Define and operationalize data Quality operating model and processes
	Identify and assess Quality of existing stores of data.	Profile, analyze critical Data against the quality dimensions, in enterprise repositories and golden sources
		Develop, extend, enrich and publish Data Quality rules
		Operationalize Data Quality monitoring
		Plan, prioritize and operationalize Data quality remediation.
	Monitor Analyze, Monitor and Report Quality of new data.	Implement Data Quality controls across the entire lifecycle of data
		Profile and analyze New data (internal and external) and store profiles stored in a central repository
		Invoke remediation for new data in error
		Develop and publish sourcing agreements with thresholds
		Audit Data Quality processes

Table 3.10: Data Quality Management

There would be some level of in-formalized processes for data management, data quality, and metadata in the organizations. Most of these processes would be in silos and need not be consistent. These informal processes documented in current state analyses should also be leveraged while re-discovering and standardizing them. The processes in Table 3.6 to Table 3.10 are level-1 processes that can be used for guidance while setting up data management services. Data quality and metadata are major dimensions of data management. It is required to align operational data management and governance processes to these dimensional services. Further chapters will provide more details on setting up and ope-rationalizing services for metadata and data quality.

Summary

Getting to understand, where the organization should be in next two years, will allow stakeholders in developing required business needs enabled by capabilities of data management, along with improvements required to existing capabilities. The target state data control environment can be depicted in a maturity model to make it much easier to communicate to the stakeholders and leadership. There may be changes required to the organizational structure, people, process and technology capabilities to facilitate the implementation of target control environment. To mature the data operations, a new operating model customized to the culture of the organization is always required. Further, the roles, responsibilities and accountabilities of stakeholders, councils and working groups need to be assigned, enabled and empowered. This can be followed by definition, standardization of processes and taking them to implementation and continuous improvement. And finally, comes the plan to assess and monitor the data management and governance activities in the organization.

4

CREATING A STANDARDIZED METADATA SERVICE

Again, I was working for a global bank, for its chief data office, based out of Bangalore. The bank headquartered in London has operations in more than 60 countries. At the same time, it has operations servicing retail, commercial, and international-banking customers. The breadth of the operations causes confusion when having to understand the data and its related context in which it is produced or applied. The bank has commissioned my services to get the data definitions captured for the discerning customer and compliance data. However, the services that existed could not assist the divisions much in obtaining the metadata.

Challenges

As I started on this engagement, I got a deep dive into the existing operating model for metadata. I see the primary challenges as follows:
1. Non-Integration between data quality, metadata and architecture dimensions
2. A federated operating model with stakeholders having difficulty accepting their responsibility to capture definitions and associated metadata
3. A meta-model that was not customized to the division, based on

its needs

4. Lagging timeboxed BCBS, financial crime programs
5. Overemphasis on formalization of data programs through policy and rigidness in data operations
6. Data stewards hired, owners enforced with responsibilities but non-existence of differentiation between responsibility and accountability

Metadata in standard terms is defined as

"a set of data that describes and gives information about other data."

National Information Standards Organization (Niso) defines it as

"structured information that describes, explains, locates, or otherwise makes it easier to retrieve, use, or manage an information resource." [5]

Is that how the Business personnel understand it?

For example, a business term *"Beneficiary"* in the context of a loan opening, need not be a participant, but in the context of a loan closure, he or she can be a participant. It is important to understand the context and the definition of the business terms from various data owners who are creating or using the same.

A data definition along with other information helps us to understand the context in which the data element is being created or used. If two words I give, Mustafa and India come straight out of a data feed, can we derive the context around it? Below is the interpretation from someone to whom I asked this question.

---

[5] Jenn R. *UNDERSTANDING METADATA, WHAT IS METADATA, AND WHAT IS IT FOR?*, Baltimore, MD: NISO

"Mustafa is the name of a person who lives in India."

However, Mustafa is the name of a store which is a corporate customer to the bank, while India is the name of a district in Singapore. As we capture the definitions for the data elements, the context gets clearer. The actual name of the district is "Little India", which got truncated to "India". This truncation which is a data quality issue will be detailed in the next chapter. Metadata thus helps an organization to understand the context in which the data is being created or used. Without metadata, the data is left for interpretation out of the context, and further implementation of changes to processes or systems will suffer as a result with inconsistent outcomes.

Challenges in Managing Data Without Metadata

- Performing a data analysis and putting data requirements when the meaning of a business element is not clear
- Building a data warehouse, or migrating a data store or integrating data from various sources would often result in myriad of questions such as "where to source data?", "what are associated delivery points?", "which transformation rules apply to the data?"
- Difficulty in understanding how the data is traversing the systems or being used as well as transformed by processes to be able to define the basic information architecture.
- Coming up with Coverage of data while implementing solutions becomes a challenge
- Unavailability of data rules stored against a data element makes it much difficult to define consistency rules and other quality rules
- Unavailability of the certified Systems of Records or References from where data can be sourced can lead to erroneous sourcing and data quality issues in the outcomes.

What is Metadata Management?

Metadata management is a series of activities ensuring that information about a business term is properly documented, when data is obtained, stored, shared, applied and destroyed. By documenting metadata, the challenges in understanding the meaning and the context of data are reduced considerably. A business analyst capturing reporting requirements need not stumble to understand what a "customer name" as a business term means in the organization. Does it also mean that the broker-dealers as well as vendors are called customers? Or should the data about these parties need to be sourced from a different business term, stored somewhere else? These questions around the content and context will be answered if information about the business term is captured as Metadata.

The organization requires technology capabilities such as standard repository that captures Business, Technical Metadata in defined templates or organized meta-models. Also, the process capabilities such as workflows and people capabilities such as authorization roles should produce metadata. All these capabilities will be used to define services which will operationalize management of metadata. Data has a life cycle, POSMAD, (Plan, Obtain, Store/Share, Maintain, Apply, and Decay) which helps in understanding the lineage better:

- Where it comes from and originates – sources?
- Which processes is it applied across?
- Who uses the business term?
- Which systems use the data element for logic?

Where does Metadata come from

Data about data does not generate by itself. Metadata needs to be sourced from many provisioning points:

- Databases
- Data warehouses
- Regulatory reports
- Management reports
- Notification reports
- Policies and procedures
- Workflow data collection
- Case tools
- Existing data dictionaries maintained in silos
- Data extraction and distribution tools
- Data Models
- Screens on systems that face users
- Physical documents
- Contractual agreements
- Application logic

Types of Metadata to be Managed

Metadata is classified into three different types such as business metadata, operational metadata and technical metadata. Table 4.1 showcases various aspects of metadata classifications.

- Business metadata management relates to active management of data definitions, relationships, sample values, domains and other aspects that provide business users with a common crowd sourced understanding of a business term.
- Operational metadata management relates to active management of administrative aspects of a business term such as ownership, stewardship, risk and privacy classifications, and entitlements. Operational metadata is also known as administrative metadata while some firms can term it as business metadata.
- Technical metadata management reates to the active management of the physical instantiation characterstics of the data elements

such as systems of truth, lineage, distribution and other physical characterstics. Technical metadata is also known as physical metadata

Further, an extensive list of attributes captured in the glossary and data dictionary in available in the metamodel section below.

Classification of Metadata	Commentary
Business Metadata	Relates to active management of data definitions, relationships, sample values, data domain, data rules to name a few attributes.
Operational Metadata	Relates to active management of data ownership, stewardship aspects, risk classification, privacy and security classification, Entitlements to name a few
Technical Metadata	Relates to active management of physical characteristics of the data element including system of record, lineage, data type, length to name a few attributes.

Table 4.1: Types of Metadata

Integrating Business and Technical Metadata

To unleash the potential of Metadata, the business metadata should be linked to operational and technical metadata. The attributes grouped under each type of metadata are available in table-14. Below is a scenario to understand the importance of this necessary integration:

1. The travel department would want to commission a report that shows flight tickets and hotel bookings generated by agents
2. The reporting business analyst gathering the requirements now

     looks for coverage of agents in customer column

3. The analyst is having difficulty identifying the data fields that have this information on agents

4. He looks for the department's glossary, in case, there is a definition of an agent. He finds that the agent, in fact, differs from a grouping known as brokers. Coming to this level of understanding would not have been possible without the locally maintained glossary. The business has discontinued the concept of agent and merged it with a broker, a year ago.

5. The analyst then looks for the data elements associated with broker, and dealer.

6. He could not find the exact names in the table columns which is a major challenge now

7. The next step is to obviously get to know from the SMEs of the system and the users to understand how this differentiation is applies while building an itinerary

8. The analyst gets to understand that customer column in-fact captures brokers as well and there is a reference data field that classifies the data element to be a customer, broker, agent or wholesaler

9. The lack of this integration between the business term and the physical instantiation of the term in the database is a major challenge for the analyst. This is one of the many challenges faced by many firms due to lack of proper definitions of data elements

10. The analyst then on further interviews with SMEs gets to update the data dictionaries for further usage in the organization with the physical data element names and their systems of records from where they can be sourced.

These challenges can be overcome by integrating the business metadata with technical metadata. Getting to understand what a business term is called in operations is as equally important as getting to understand how, where and when it is stored physically. The quality analysis and control steps that are enforced by Governance must ensure that there are no orphan technical or business metadata in the data dictionaries and completeness is ensured.

Metadata-as-a-Service

Standardizing Metadata–as–service will assist the organization in pushing or pulling the capabilities based on their needs. The data organization needs to emphasize promotion of existing metadata capabilities. This is a stepping stone when the cultural change of "Managing Data as an Asset" is to be trickled into grass roots of the firm. The awareness sessions should be customized based on the nature of stakeholder groups. One wouldn't want to pitch the word metadata to business users, operational and front end staff. As this often gives a technical fervor, I prefer to use "Business Terms" and "Associated characteristics" to refer to data elements and related Metadata.

As stated earlier, metadata does not generate information on its own and requires every responsible stakeholder, system, and process to produce Metadata consistently. It can include definitions, owners, the length of data element and the systems of record along with other aspects that characterize the context of data. Capturing metadata, further enables holistic Governance of other data dimensions such as data quality and architecture. A service comprising of repeatable metadata activities helps in active management and governance of metadata while ensuring consistent outcomes and sustainability in the organization. The service would also ensure that metadata management activities are operationalized as defined by the policy.

Metadata Service Catalog

A service catalog provides a list of activities that are encapsulated into definitive service operations. These boundaries must be used to align and arrange activities into discrete (non-overlapping) functional partitions with interfaces that are well suited for service enablement. The model in exhibit 4.1, defines the role of the Service Domain in two facades – a type of business function performed ("functional pattern") and the object that is acted on such as "Define Metadata needs for data in scope."

A best practice is to fulfill the asset life cycle that starts with "Metadata scoping" and ends with "Metadata management" as shown in Table 4.2 below.

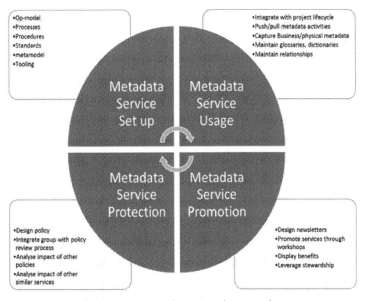

Exhibit 4.1: Metadata Service Catalog

Metadata Management Integrated with Software Development Lifecycle

Metadata management also has a lifecycle that needs to be aligned with project Management, transformation and risk management lifecycle stages. But, is your firm actively managing the status of the metadata across its lifecycle to manage the metadata itself? In Exhibit 4.2, there is a visual snapshot on the statistics of metadata status across its lifecycle, viewed from the perspectives of domain, system, process, and user. For example, the Data Domain-A, 50% of data elements or business terms have been defined while only 30% are published.

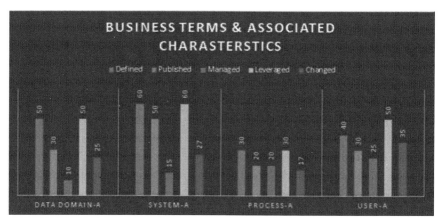

Exhibit 4.2: Status of Metadata in its lifecycle as viewed from a domain, system, process and user.

Further, each metadata phase like "Scoping" or "Capture metadata needs" is to be mapped to Waterfall, Agile and Business transformation life-cycle stages for better maintainability and governance. A sample mapping of metadata stages to Software Development Lifecycle stages are, as shown in Table 4.2.

Service Phase	Software Development Lifecycle Phase	Metadata Phase
Service Promotion	Project planning Business analysis planning	Metadata scoping
Service Usage	Requirement analysis	Business Metadata capture
Service Usage	Design Build	Technical Metadata capture Lineage capture
Service Usage	Testing	Validate Metadata
Service Usage	Post implementation	Manage Metadata

Table 4.2: Metadata lifecycle integrated with SDLC stages

At the outset, Metadata is enabled by namespaces that are logical placeholders that hold required information in defined templates.

Metadata repositories — Namespace that stores, publishes and shares metadata along with the relationships. People can leverage metadata stored in repositories during the requirement, data analysis, design and other phases of a change life cycle

Data dictionary — Namespace that holds business terms along with their associated definitions. Data Dictionaries will as well contain business, operational and technical metadata

Data Glossary — Namespace that holds terms of reference used in descriptions along with acronyms and alternate names

Data lineage — Attributes of a data element that have details on the data provider, systems to which data is distributed, systems in which data is stored and decayed. It also showcases the processes as data traverses across systems.

Rules management — Namespace that holds data rules including data quality rules, policy enforcement rules, transformation rules, derivation rules, notification rules, threshold rules about a data element.

Taxonomies — Namespace that supports entity-relationship (ER) models, ontology and other data modeling, and relationships.

Meta-model and Structure

It is necessary to understand the relations between data assets to manage them better. The aspects detailed in Table 4.3, form the core structure to define a metamodel. It leads me to identify the aspects of an asset, attributes, and relationship

Aspect	Description
Asset	An asset is the lowest level of piece of data, which can be managed as a single entity
Domain	Is a logical collection of assets into Glossaries, Dictionaries, Data Quality rules, etc
Attribute	Similar to a data model, an asset like a data element can have attributes like the definition, data domain, dataset, data owner, etc.
Relationship	The asset can hold a relationship with another asset like a synonym, acronym.

Table 4.3: A description of a high level metamodel

Structuring Data

The challenge for organizations has always been to harmonize disparate data across the organizations' landscape or a business function. This is because data is referred to with different names, interpreted in different meaning, in a same division or firm. Classifying data into semantic, logical and physical models helps in deriving ownership at a high level as shown in Table-10.

Semantics refer to the adoption of precise, shared and consistent and open ended business meaning of data across the enterprise. This is what "managing data as a meaning" emphasizes. Does a customer mean

"The person who is opting for financial services from the bank"

or

> *"does it also include the brokers, Beneficiaries of an account as well?" "Does it really depend on the context such as an account opening in which a beneficiary is considered a customer?"*

The inconsistency in understanding data has been primarily due to the in-organic growth of organizations and their processes. This has been stemming from the non-existence of planning for data management during mergers, acquisitions, and organizational growth. To move away from these challenges, Semantics is a boon, which is a discipline of assigning unambiguous meaning to data. Semantics are usually associated with Business Architecture where a *Business object* is used to represent significant informational and conceptual elements in business context. The other way of referring to a *Business Object* is that it is a passive entity that represents business, products or services in context.

Techniques like Semantic modeling, Business Metadata management, Logical classification of data, as shown in Table 4.4, along with Data Entity views can be leveraged to capture precise, consistent and open ended definitions. These techniques will further aid in simplification of the landscape. Further simplification can be achieved by breaking down the landscape into logical classifications such as Customer or Finance domain and further classifying into datasets such as "customer product transactions" or "customer demography". Also, data can be classified based on physical characteristics such as master, reference or transaction data for better management based on their characteristics.

A Conceptual level describes data in its highest form, identifying *things* required to satisfy business objectives while also defining the relationships with other *things*. In Business architecture, *Business Object* is a passive entity that represents business entity, product or service in its context. The passive counterpart of *Business Object* in business architecture, is the *Data Object, at the level of* Application architecture. Techniques like logical models, business metadata for business terms, are used to capture precise, consistent definitions of data objects.

The logical level is a fully attributed conceptual model that is abstracted from physical instantiation of data. The logical model represents business requirements in terms of what is needed to satisfy the objectives of the business function. It can also be associated with the *Data objects* at the Application Architecture. Techniques like logical models, business metadata for data elements, can be used to capture precise, consistent definitions of data objects and its attributes.

The Physical level is the instantiation of meaning, relationships and attributes of data at a physical level in a database or storage devices. Physical models are usually attributed to the Technology Architecture. A physical piece of data is called a *Data Artifact* as is produced, consumed or stored by the software applications. It models typical messages, extracts, scripts, database tables, and documents. Example – A Lead campaign extract.

Data Classification levels	Standard definitions	Lineage (L) Relationship(R)	Usage	Techniques	Examples
Semantic	Business Term	Business Term to Logical data element name (L) Business Term to Business Term (R)	Common business language used in firm. Usually, the business vocabulary used by operations, regulatory or legal groups, common language used in industry	Semantic model Conceptual model Taxonomy Ontology	Product Name – Legal Product Name – Contractual Product Name – Sales Product Name – Regulatory filings
Logical	Logical Data Element Name Or Business name	Logical data element to Physical data element (L) Logical data element to Logical Data element (R)	Data in Business Intelligence platforms, Data mappings, local glossaries, reports	Logical Model Data Dictionary Glossary Data Directory Data Book	Savings Account – Short Name checking Account – Long Name Savings Account - Temenos
Physical	Physical Data Element Name Or System name	Physical data element name to physical data element name (R)	Names used in physical data structures	Physical data structures Databases Physical data models Canonical models	Svgsname Acctype

Table 4.4: Semantic, Logical and Physical Models

A meta-model defines standard attributes that represent the charac-teristics which need to be captured to manage and govern data unique to each abstraction level. The template that is used to obtain metadata will have containers for Semantic, conceptual, logical and physical elements to be captured and maintained.

The Meta-model is customized and aligned to Metadata operating model, based on the needs and objectives of data management and organization. New technology capabilities will be implemented or existing ones improved to accommodate the meta-model in metadata daily operations.

Quoting an example: at a conceptual level, a data element is known as a business term. The metadata associated with a business term includes data definition, synonym, alternate name, data domain, data concept, sample values to name a few attributes. This metadata is called business metadata. An example can be a "product name".

At a logical level, a business term is called a logical data element and the informational attributes include description of data element, synonyms, conceptual representation of the logical name, sample values to name a few. An example can be an "investment account - long name"

Based, on the asset type, say a Business term at conceptual level or Data Element at the logical or physical level, the attributes can be made as mandatory or nonmandatory. The meta-model further defines the structural requirements of physical data element including the data type, length, table, column, and relationship to other asset types.

Relationships between Business terms/Data elements

Mapping relationships between the business terms and data elements in-fact simplifies the data landscape. It is a best practice to capture all the relationships associated with the data that will aid in better impact analysis, data analysis and requirement management. Every change in state of an entity like a "Lead to Customer" is associated with business rules like "A lead on completing a product purchase transaction is a customer". Further, if there is a business rule that has multiple business terms, the business terms appearing in the rule can be related with a relationship like "Relates to" after importing them to Glossary. Sample relationship types are available in the Table 4.5 below.

Relationship Type	Commentary
Calculates from	Refers to terms from which current term is derived
Relates to	Refers to terms that are related to current term (can be a complex relationship like a transformation rule or a business rule)
Specializes	Refers to terms for which current term provides a more specific definition
Synonym	Refers to terms that are equivalent to the current term (simple equivalent or synonym)
Governed by	Terms that belong to the domain and dataset (Already captured)
Inheritance	For role based relationships that inherit properties of parent entity
Acronyms	Abbreviated form of business term used in organization
Groups	Business term group that cluster multiple business terms/data elements logically
Contributor	The logically classified domain or dataset in which the business term is edited or context is provided
Viewer	The logically classified domain or dataset along with context in which the business term is applied.

Table 4.5: Relationship Types between Business Terms

Meta-model

A Metamodel in simple sense is a template that is used to organize Metadata. There can be various sections like Business, Operational and Technical Metadata along with attributes that hold the information associated with the data element. A sample Meta-model for business, operational and technical metadata that captures the essential attributes about data are shown in Table 4.6, Table 4.7, Table 4.8 below.

Metadata Type	Attribute	Description
Business Metadata	Business Term	The representation of an entity or a thing or it's characteristics at a conceptual level
	Definition	Definition of the data element in simple, concise statement in context of the business process without stating what it is not.
	Synonym	The word having the same or nearly the same meaning as Business term
	Synonym of	If this Business term is in-fact a synonym of other business term, the element refers to the same
	Acronym	an abbreviation formed from the initial letters of other words and pronounced as a word
	Authoritative Data Source	Is the authoritative system of record that holds the most accurate data
	Data Domain	Logical classification of business terms termed as a domain like customer or product
	Dataset/Data Concept	Further logical classification of a business terms in a domain like interest rate condition
	Reference data classification	The data element if it classifies other data, and has a control vocabulary
	Current standard	The current reference data standard
	Future Reference data standard	If a global standard exist for this data, the same will be captured here
	Product Association	The products that the business term is associated with
	Customer Association	The type of customers that the business term is associated with
	Business Rules	The business rules that enforce constraints on data to process a condition or logic
	Associated calculations	The calculations associated with the business term
	Comments	Any additional comments that cannot be captured in Definitions

Table 4.6: The metamodel – Business Metadata attributes

76

Metadata Type	Attribute	Description
Operational Metadata	Privacy Classification	The privacy classification associated with the business term like "Highly sensitive customer data" or "Sensitive employee data"
	Data Owner	The owner for this piece of data who is accountable
	Contributing Data Domain Owner	The data owner for the domain that is considered the owning domain like customer
	Applying Data Domain owner	The data owner of a domain that consumes this data element for a function like finance
	Security Classification	The security classification associated with the data element like "Restricted"
	Access Rights	The accesses that apply to this data element without request
	Data Lifecycle controls	The control requirements across lifecycle stages of data like restriction to store

Table 4.7: The metamodel – Operational Metadata attributes

Metadata Type	Attribute	Description
Technical Metadata	Data Element	The physical instantiation of the Business term in a database or Data warehouse
	System of Record	The authoritative system of truth
	System of Reference	The golden copy of the system of truth
	Allowable Values	The list of control vocabulary or allowable values for a business term like country codes or Loan status
	Data Quality Requirements	The technical data quality requirements
	Applicable data quality dimensions	The dimensions of data quality like completeness or validity associated with the data quality requirements
	Thresholds	The thresholds for each of the data quality requirements
	Transformation rules	The rules used for transformation that includes the data element
	Derivation rules	The rules used to derive the data element
	Source Data Base	This is a lineage concept, the source from which the data is extracted to distribute
	Source Table	This is a lineage concept, the source table from which data is extracted to distribute
	Source Schema	This is a lineage concept, the source schema from which data is extracted to distribute
	Target Database	This is a lineage concept, the target database to which data is distributed
	Target table	This is a lineage concept, the target table to which data is distributed
	Target Schema	This is a lineage concept, the target schema to which data is distributed
	Extract Name	This is a lineage concept, the extract that is used to distribute data from source to target
	Extract load Time	This is a lineage concept, the load time of the extract to target database
	Load Frequency	This is a lineage concept, the frequency at which the target database is loaded
	Data Type	The type of the data element like numeric
	Nullable	The element captures the nullability allowed characteristics as binary yes or no
	Precision	If the data element is numeric, the decimals allowed
	Min	The minimum value associated with the data element
	Max	The maximum value associated with data element
	Canonical Name	If using data services like Enterprise service bus, the canonical name associated with the data element
	Canonical Group	If using data services like Enterprise service bus, the canonical classification name associated with the data element

Table 4.8: The metamodel – Technical Metadata attributes

Simplifying Data landscape using custom Information Model

As long as a data landscape stands complex to the understanding of common stakeholders, it does not assist the growth of the organization. The first activity in simplifying the landscape is to identify logical and physical domains and datasets. For example, the logical classification for any industry would be Customer and Finance domains that hold data related to the customer and finance operations.

Physical domains are defined based on physical characteristics such as master, reference and transaction data. This, in fact, satisfies the need to manage data based on the physical characteristics and pace with which data changes. It will also create clear boundaries based on better understanding of ownership of data. Thus, the high-level classification of business areas into data domains is the first step to simplification.

There are two approaches to simplify a data domain further into logical entities called concepts or data sets. This can be done by:

1. logically breaking down the data domain into datasets
2. Grouping data into an associated dataset or concept
3. Generalization and specialization of an existing concept

Approach 1

For each concept, identify a suitable name that defines it such as "Interest rate condition"

Ø put the definition in a dictionary, and use this definition to represent the concept

Note: Add properties and restrictions as applicable

Approach 2

To support industry-specific concepts for banking (BIAN standards, FIBO, MISMO), arrive at an elevated level abstract concept already defined in these models. These concepts represent *things* using set-theory. But, under these concepts, the specialized concepts can be defined, based on the need. FIBO Concepts for Party Data can include buyers, sellers, customers, clients while a specialization of these concepts can include Broker-Dealer, Registered Independent Advisor, Wholesaler, Beneficiary. The specialization of concepts defines the facts applicable to the thing and transitions slowly to closed world assumption of how business represents data.

Ø Think of a suitable label which could reasonably label the sub-classification of data lower than a domain

Techniques

1. Class modeling
2. Business Landscape modeling
3. Service modeling
4. Ontologies and taxonomies modeling

Functional Standards

1. FIBO
2. BIAN
3. MISMO

Metadata Naming Standards

The best practices and guidelines to standardizing data elements or business terms can be customized from the Industry standards including ISO 11179. A data element naming can be of the following formats for brevity and consistency:

- **Object** [*Qualifier*] Property Representation Term
- [**Concept**] <*Qualifier*> Class

Further, considerations while naming a data element or a business term are below:

- "<>" for Qualifier are optional
- The Concept can be captured along with the data domain in data dictionary as well
- For example: [**Import Loan Facility**] <*Last Paid*> Installment Amount

A sample set of standards to define a data element should:

1. be stated in the singular
2. state what the data element is and should not specify what it is not
3. be stated as a descriptive phrase or sentence(s)
4. contain only commonly understood abbreviations
5. be expressed without embedding definitions of other data elements or concepts

Technology and Infrastructure

Based on the requirements set forth for Technology and Infrastructure, a decision needs to be taken for a build vs. buy. If the choice is to buy, a vendor analysis can be initiated to cater to the core and the additional capabilities required in collecting, integrating and actively managing Metadata. An organization in its initial state of maturity would just have started managing metadata but could decide on having to pace with metadata capture using innovative tagging features. Or, it can go with a choice of having to mature slowly by opting with basic capabilities of capturing metadata using data analysts. If existing technology capabilities are to be customized to host a metadata repository, the system may impose technical constraints on the design of the solution. These may include development languages, hardware and software platforms, connectivity to third party applications, Integration services, application software, data stores that must be used.

It is a fact that Metadata management drives Governance and it is also required to govern Metadata. Business metadata like domains and Operational metadata like data owner play an active role in Governing data across the organization. While Business metadata like the business term and technical metadata like source and target databases direct active data management. To manage and govern Metadata actively, the people and process capabilities like workflows and organizational structure should be imbibed into operating model and associated metadata processes. The meta-models, processes, environments, organization structure and workflow in a metadata management solution must be customized based on the defined operating model.

The sponsor can go with a buy vs. build decision as stated earlier, given the capabilities that the firm requires and the outcomes they desire. If it a build decision, a combination of database platforms, ETL tools, BI tools along with EAI tools can be used to develop a metadata management solution. There are firms which started off by customizing such an in-house solution to cater to capture and management of Metadata. As they matured in capturing metadata, they now started to realize the needs of actively managing and governing metadata. They, in fact, are migrating to vendor based solutions given the features like nimbleness to customize, self-service, workflow, non-cluttering and ease of use. A generic architecture for a metadata management solution is presented in Exhibit 4.3.

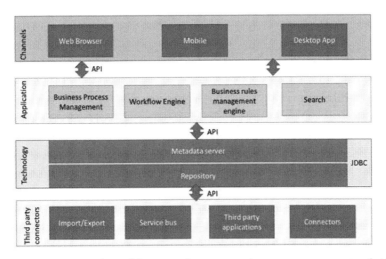

Exhibit 4.3: Generic architecture for a metadata management solution

From this chapter, it is understandable that Metadata Management as a practice is making strides in the financial industry assisting realization of Benefits; a favorite question in the Governance industry is ""Should governance and metadata work in tandem to realize the benefits?" While there is a need to manage and govern metadata, it enables Governance in the organization. Metadata enables policy associated with Data Sourcing, Data Usage, Data Security and Privacy, Risk, Architecture, and Data Quality.

Interdependence between Metadata and Governance functions

How does Governance enable Metadata?

Metadata management also requires capturing characteristics of data at the right stage of the change (change as a project/program) by including the right stakeholders, consistently. This can be enabled by data governance guaranteeing that metadata is collected by project stakeholders, in coordination with data owners enforced by data stewardship.

How does Metadata enable Governance?

Business Metadata management relates to management of definitions, relationships, and business rules while operational metadata relates to active management of assigned data owners, risk classification, controls around data life-cycle, entitlements and other administrative aspects. Various other administrative aspects aiding governance, include contributing and viewing data domains as well as stewards.

Recently, there was a discussion in a forum – "Is it Data Quality or Governance that is a priority?" Well, both the dimensions need to be synchronized, to realize the benefits that either data quality or metadata Management or Governance provide. The industry should start understanding the importance and clear delineation between each of the dimensions to orchestrate data management and governance dimensions with efficiency, sustainability, and benefits management.

Summary

Metadata is "data about data," and this information can be managed through a series of repeatable activities like metadata capture, integration and active management. As organizations are in a state of standardizing these metadata management processes, it is necessary to attain maturity and consistency through service set-up and operationalizing metadata-as-a-service. The distributed divisions that passively document metadata in glossaries are now enabled to pull these services, at the right phase of a change management lifecycle. This enables the organization as an whole in standardizing data as a meaning, defining relationships and understanding where the data is created, stored, applied and deleted which is treasure trove of information to simplify the data landscape.

5

RUNNING A DATA QUALITY SERVICE

When an organization widely explores the benefits of standardizing data quality-as-a-service, they look to find efficiency and scalability in their data quality operations. At the same time, the industry standards including DAMA, EDM, and COBIT provide best practices and guidelines to start standardizing the data quality management activities. An organization adopting and implementing a framework that has the dimensions of quality including validity, consistency, completeness, accuracy and others is not much of a challenge but maturing across data quality operations, while making it sustainable is a challenge today for most firms.

Which data should be monitored for quality?

Identifying the critical or key data elements should be at the forefront of the data quality assessment and monitoring activities. Table 10, shows a sample framework using the data characterstics of risk, value, privacy and management to force-score the data elements to arrive at an objective score. The combination of the score and thresholds will be used to arrive at the key or critical data classifications. The data elements can either be classified as critical data elements or as level 1, 2, ..N data elements. When data is classified into levels, based on the need, it is usually classified into 3 or 4 levels as required. This priority classification is the foundation to have the focus on data that requires active management. Based on the needs, the level 1 key data elements (scored above Median threshold) can be managed for quality by a central data quality function. While the level 2 can be managed by the business unit's distributed data quality management functions, while level 3 can be prioritized and managed by business unit, based on the impact.

Weightage	10	7	10	7	7	10	10	7
Criteria	Risk		Value				Privacy	Characteristics
Classification	Regulatory Risk (Low = 4, Medium = 7, high = 10)	Operational Risk (Low = 4, Medium = 7, high = 10)	Critical in > 1 Business Unit (<1 BU = 4, 2 BU = 7, >2 = 10)	Used in Financial calculations (1 calc = 4, 10 calc = 7, >10 calc =10)	Used in Reporting (1 report = 4, 10 report = 7, >10 report =10)	Number of Incidents (1 = 4, 5 = 7, >10 = 10)	Privacy classification (Internal = 4, Restricted = 7, Highly Restricted = 10)	Transaction = 4, Master = 7, Reference =10
Data Element - 1								
Data Element - n								
Score								

Table 5.1: Risk & Value Realization framework

Defining Data Rules holistically

Business rules are an integral component of consistency quality checks and are often ignored in operational data quality processes which are implemented by business data stewards, data owners and data quality analysts. A business rule can be a consistency rule when viewed from a perspective of data distributed between end points. A loan can have a status of "Loss Mitigation" in a servicing system while the same loan in Enterprise Resource Planning system (ERP) can show as "In Servicing". This is a lack of consistency in the same piece of data. It is not only the business rules that have specific use in data quality but, other data rules also add to the holistic definition of rules as well. Data is the life plasma of the business functions; business rules define how the organizational policies and decisions are enforced by leveraging data through rules. Data Rules thus channelize the active functioning of an organization. The various data rules that should be captured with clear delineation to manage data quality better are shown in Table 11.

Business Rules Classification
Decision rules by which the business derives the conclusions from conditions.
o e.g. For a value, inference and conclusion from business
Data Rules that define the precise characteristics that data needs to adhere to
o e.g. valid values or ranges for particular fields, relationships between fields or records, etc.
Target Rules that define the thresholds for Data Quality Indicators
o e.g. red-amber-green status (for health check based on thresholds, will be used for representation in scorecards, dashboards)
Notification Rules that define alerts that should be triggered under particular circumstances
o e.g. notifying a data steward if a record fails a validation check, alerting a data owner if data quality falls below a defined threshold, etc
Transformation/Derivation Rules that define operations that should be applied to data.
o e.g. logic establishing the conditions under which one statement can be derived or validly deduced from one or more other statements
Policy enforcement rules
o Defines constraints on process/functions using data that is based on policy

Table 5.2: Data Rules Classification

The policy enforcement and the business rules will be realized as data consistency and validity data rules. To quote an example of a consistency rule, a country code for a customer address in California can be a GPO code like Calif., in a system while it needs to be a ISO code like US-CA, as enforced by policy or reference data standards.

The semantic equivalency of the State code is same though it is an ISO or a GPO standard. But, the structural consistency for the context of the business term is lacking in this scenario. This often leads to increased costs of maintaining redundant values associated with the same business term that also increases complexity in integration and application of data.

Similarly, a product code "50" can relate to a product A in the product management application while the product code of 50 in another reconciliation system means product B. This is an example of semantic non-equivalence of data.

Quoting another example: the status of the customer can be "Active" while the status of the same customer in a marketing application can show as "Closed". It is necessary to check where these is a wanted redundancy of data across the landscape. The data dictionaries and the glossary will provide information on where the same business term is maintained physically across various data stores. The next step is to validate the scope of the remediation required.

In Table 12 is sample illustration for a broker segment, on grouping business rules, (*decision rules*) from multiple logic statements into a two-dimensional tabular view. It is much easier to manage and scale rules for data quality when they are managed as metadata. I was crowd-sourcing and eliciting ideas on better management of data rules in the IIBA group that aids better management of data.

Element Name	Conditions					Conclusions		
Broker Segment	Sales		Frequency of consistent sales in years	1st sale date		Derivation/ Transformation	Business Rule (Conclusion on product sales)	Data Rules
Segment-A	Is Greater than	$10M	10	Is greater than	11 Years	Platinum	May sell/Will be	All products at $10M level	Valid Values for Broker segment are Segment-A, Segment-B, Platinum, Gold, Silver, New Broker
	Is Greater than	$10M	5	Is greater than	6 Years	Gold	May sell/ Will be	5 products at $10M level	
	Is Greater than	$10M	1	Is greater than	0.6 Years	Silver	May sell/ will be	only one product at the $10M LEVEL	
Segment – B		$0M		Is Less than	0.6 Years	New Broker	May sell/ will be	In the same segment for 6 months. promoted based on sales, in 7th month	

Table 5.3: Decision Rules Illustration

Every change in the state of an entity like a "lead" to a "customer" is associated with business rules like *"A lead on completing a product purchase transaction is a customer."* If a business rule has multiple business terms forming the rule, these participating business terms appearing in the rule can be partnered with a relationship attribute like "Relates to" in the data dictionary.

Defining a Target Data Quality Operating model

Most of the organizations are fairly maturing their data management and governance capabilities to meet their end goals. For example, data quality activities would have been started by the IT division based on the *"then needs"* like reducing data related risks and meeting regulatory needs. But, the recent organizational drivers requiring *"Managing data as a meaning"*, *"Customer Excellence" and "Data Risk management"* is pushing the need for alignment of data quality management and other dimensions to the risk management and corporate governance structure. A sample target state environment for data quality that integrates other data management and governance dimensions are highlighted in Exhibit 5.1 below.

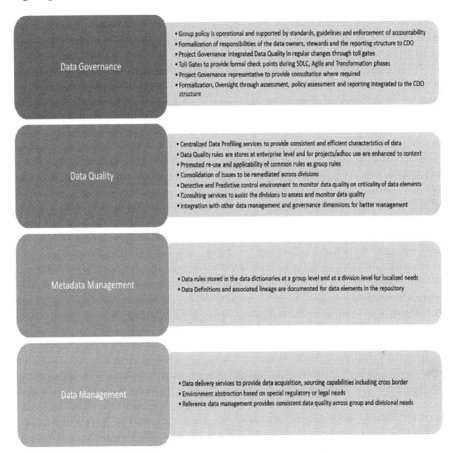

Exhibit 5.1: Target State environment for Data Quality Management & integration with Governance

Organizational Structure and Culture

The formal and informal working relationships that exist within the enterprise may need to change to facilitate the desired future state. Sample stakeholder and stakeholder groups in a future state are described in Exhibit 5.2. Changes to the reporting lines of business data stewards can encourage business and operations teams to work more closely with business operations while facilitating alignment to their quality goals. Elements of the organizational structure and culture may need to change to support the future state.

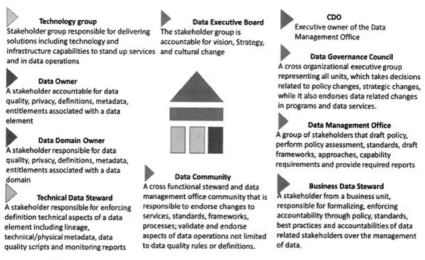

Technology group
Stakeholder group responsible for delivering solutions including technology and infrastructure capabilities to stand up services and in data operations

Data Owner
A stakeholder accountable for data quality, privacy, definitions, metadata, entitlements associated with a data element

Data Domain Owner
A stakeholder responsible for data quality, privacy, definitions, metadata, entitlements associated with a data domain

Technical Data Steward
A stakeholder responsible for enforcing definition technical aspects of a data element including lineage, technical/physical metadata, data quality scripts and monitoring reports

Data Executive Board
The stakeholder group is accountable for vision, Strategy, and cultural change

Data Community
A cross functional steward and data management office community that is responsible to endorse changes to services, standards, frameworks, processes; validate and endorse aspects of data operations not limited to data quality rules or definitions.

CDO
Executive owner of the Data Management Office

Data Governance Council
A cross organizational executive group representing all units, which takes decisions related to policy changes, strategic changes, while it also endorses data related changes in programs and data services.

Data Management Office
A group of stakeholders that draft policy, perform policy assessment, standards, draft frameworks, approaches, capability requirements and provide required reports

Business Data Steward
A stakeholder from a business unit, responsible for formalizing, enforcing accountability through policy, standards, best practices and accountabilities of data related stakeholders over the management of data.

Exhibit 5.2: Organizational Structure for Data Quality Services

Note: Data stewardship roles should be standardized for alignment either across business units or across geographies (in case of a difference in operations across the globe)

Defining Data Quality Specific Roles

To have a data quality service functioning, specific roles, as stated in the Exhibit 5.3 are required to be defined and assigned.

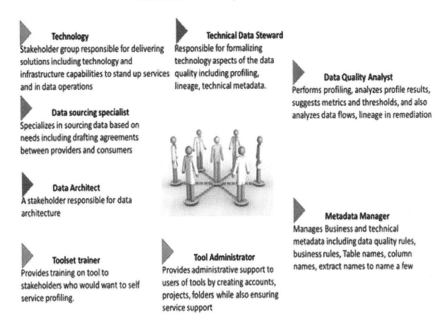

Technology
Stakeholder group responsible for delivering solutions including technology and infrastructure capabilities to stand up services and in data operations

Data sourcing specialist
Specializes in sourcing data based on needs including drafting agreements between providers and consumers

Data Architect
A stakeholder responsible for data architecture

Toolset trainer
Provides training on tool to stakeholders who would want to self service profiling.

Technical Data Steward
Responsible for formalizing technology aspects of the data quality including profiling, lineage, technical metadata.

Tool Administrator
Provides administrative support to users of tools by creating accounts, projects, folders while also ensuring service support

Data Quality Analyst
Performs profiling, analyzes profile results, suggests metrics and thresholds, and also analyzes data flows, lineage in remediation

Metadata Manager
Manages Business and technical metadata including data quality rules, business rules, Table names, column names, extract names to name a few

Exhibit 5.3: Data Quality specific roles and Responsibilities

It is required to formalize these roles and integrate it into daily data operations in such a way that these services are no longer perceived as an overhead. This is one of the major challenges that the organizations are facing today.

Challenges in Adoption of Data Quality Management

Further challenges that most organizations are facing today in orchestrating data quality management are detailed below:

1. *Challenges in the cultural adoption* of data risk management, in a distributed way in the organization is a major challenge. Most of the organizations take a value-based approach to data quality management but fail to realize that a risk-based approach is also required, in the interest of enterprise goals.

2. *Awareness of data quality services* is a major challenge in enterprises. With awareness comes adoption and enablement in organization to embrace data quality services.

3. *Project governance* structure along with required artifacts and deliverables at every stage, in a project life cycle, would have already been defined. One such activity can be providing data definitions and business metadata in the business requirements documents (BRD) for data that is in scope for project. This has *a limited adoption* and needs to be enforced through data governance, risk management, and project-management-office (PMO) integration.

4. There is a need for continuous enhancement of data quality services, operating model, and thresholds to complement the current needs of stakeholders, organizations and challenges.

Data-Quality-Management-as-a-Service

Most challenges can be overcome by re-discovering and standardizing the current data quality management activities into regular data operations. There is a need for a target operating model (TOM) that consists of discrete functional modules that collaborate through service calls. Each governance function can be considered as a **Governance Area** as shown in Exhibit 5.4, to orchestrate coherent activities within a **service domain** called the **service operation**. Service operations describe a high-level dependency in a Service Domain or between two service domains.

1. **Data Governance Area** – is the highest-level classification of the governance domain. An area groups a set of business processes and technology capabilities to achieve an end goal for data management. Data Quality for example is a governance area

2. **Service Domain** – is the finest level of partitioning, each defining unique, discrete business, process, and technology capabilities.

The service domains are the elemental building blocks of a data governance service landscape. Examples of service domains are Service Usage and Service protection.

3. *Service Operation* – is an important collaborative function that describes what business, process or technology functionality it should contain and what functionality it needs to access through delegated service operation calls to other service areas and service domains. Usually, this would be through a combination of functional pattern and an asset in focus.

A data quality service can be well defined with a set of service domains including service setup, service promotion, service usage, service protection, service monitoring and improvement.

Exhibit 5.4: Data Quality Service catalog

The following example from data quality service, the service domain *"Data Quality Service Set-Up"* in Table 5.4, details the service operations including the functional pattern and the asset. Quoting an example from data quality service, the service domain *"Data Quality service setup"* in the below model details the Service operations including functional pattern and Asset.

Service Phase	Service ID	Functional Pattern	Asset	Operation Description
Data Quality Service Set up	SS1.1	Plan	Strategy	Develop DQ strategy and design approach
Data Quality Service Set up	SS1.2	Communicate	Strategy	Communicate strategy to relevant stakeholders, councils, committees, leadership
Data Quality Service Set up	SS1.3	Plan	Operating Model	Plan operational processes and Develop an operating model
Data Quality Service Set up	SS1.4	Communicate	Operating Model	Communicate Operating model to relevant stakeholders, councils, committees, leadership, stewards and owners
Data Quality Service Set up	SS1.5	Administer	Feedback Solicitation	Solicit and incorporate feedback into the strategy and operating model
Data Quality	SS1.6	Endorse	Strategy and operating model	Stakeholders and management

Table 5.4: Data Quality Service SetUp

Alignment of Services with COBIT Framework

COBIT provides an Industry-accepted framework. Once implemented, the executives can ensure that data governance is aligned effectively with business enterprise goals and also better directs the use of data for the business's advantage. COBIT provides best practices, control activities and tools for assessment, monitoring, and governing data quality management (IT) activities. COBIT processes can be mapped to service domains to clearly differentiate management from governance as shown in Table 5.5.

Dimensions	Description	Sub Dimension
Accuracy	Refers to the degree that the value represents a real life entities they model	
Completeness	Availability of required data attributes and records	Count of Records
		Frequency distribution
		Fill rate
Consistency	Ensuring values in one dataset are consistent with another	Record consistency
		Structural consistency
		Semantic Consistency
		Pattern Analysis
Currency	Degree to which information is current to be applied	
Precision	Level of details on the characteristics of data elements	
Reasonableness	Level of consistency in operational context	
Referential Integrity	Condition that exists when all intended references from data in one column of a table to data in another column of same or different table	
Timeliness	Expectation of availability of the data by specified interval	Manual Float
		System Float
Uniqueness	No entity exists more than once	Duplicacy
		Redundancy
Validity	Ensures data values confirm to numerous characteristics like range of values	Range of Values
		Decimals
		Content check

Table 5.5: COBIT Practices mapped to Data Quality service Catalog

The existing data quality capabilities at a lower level will be standard-ized into discrete functional modules. The focus on implementing the current capabilities can be in the order stated in Exhibit 5.5 below.

99

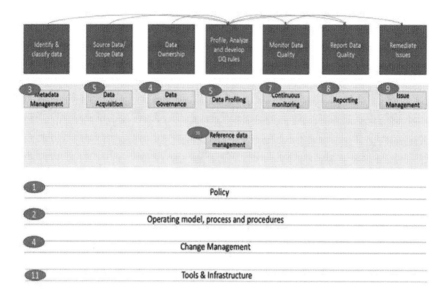

Exhibit 5.5: High-Level Capabilities grouped for implementation in order

Processes to set-up and Ope-rationalize the Data Quality Service

The high-level processes to setup and ope-rationalize data quality are quoted in Table 5.6 below. Efficient processes that are lean and provide consistent outcomes are required for data quality management.

Data Management activities	Capabilities
Data quality program is established	The data quality strategy, target state objectives and approach is defined, communicated and endorsed
	Accountable parties have been identified and roles and responsibilities have been assigned.
	Data Quality operating model and processes are defined, and operational
Quality of existing stores of data are identified and assessed.	Data is profiled, analyzed and described for Data Quality against the dimensions, in enterprise repositories and golden sources
	Data Quality rules are extended, enriched and published
	Data Quality monitoring is operational
	Data quality remediation has been planned, prioritized and actioned.
Quality of new data is monitored, analyzed and reported	Data Quality controls are in place across the entire lifecycle of data
	New data (internal and external) is profiled and profiles stored in a central repository
	Remediation is invoked for data in error
	Data Quality processes are audited by risk function

Table 5.6: Data Quality Processes along with activity descriptions

New or improved processes can be implemented by leveraging existing or new target state organizational structure. The processes at a high level are available as shown in Table 5.7 below.

Process (L1)	Description
Initial Engagement	Determine the scope, needs, and skills available in the business unit for Data Quality assessment and management
Define Data Requirements	Provide critical data elements to be sourced for profiling. Further provide format and the type in which data will be presented along with physical data structure information like schema, tables.
Metadata Input	Also provide business definition, schema, database, column, extract details and required technical information
Access to Data	Understand the constraints and availability of data for profiling
Source Data	If Access to data is restricted, source data with agreements
User Access	Provide access to analysts to profile data in the tool. This can be a one time activity
Profile Data	Understand the characteristics of Data is the staging environment by profiling
Identify potential Issues	The characteristics of data are analyzed to identify potential issues
Rule development	The data quality rules are developed including completeness, consistency, accuracy, and timeliness
Execute rules	Run data quality rules against data
Review rules	From the initial results of rules run, tweak the rules to attain necessary results
Publish rules	Publish the rules in the enterprise repository to be leveraged across the enterprise
Manage rules	Data rules are managed regularly based on need or whenever the profile of data changes
Schedule rules run	Schedule continuous run of rules to monitor data quality at regular intervals
Notify Issues	Provide timely reports to stakeholders including data owners, stewards and other responsible personnel.
Remediate Issues	Prioritize and fix the data quality issues high up in the lifecycle preferably in system of record or deploy maintenance to systems and processes to fix the issues.

Table 5.7: Level-1 Data Quality Processes and Descriptions

The data owner, business data steward, project business analyst or data management office has a need to understand the characteristics of data. The technical data stewards can be engaged by business data stewards to determine the type of engagement that is required with the division, based on the availability of the skills. The business unit has a need for assistance in sourcing data from a provisioning point but not with profiling data and developing quality rules. The skills missing are assessed and the central service is engaged for data provisioning from System of Record or Reference.

Data Quality Exploration and Analysis

A firm needs to understand where the quality of its data is lacking. It is also important to understand where the data is being applied, as it helps the firms to understand an estimate on impact of poor data quality. It is important to know where the data is created or produced to have it corrected at the system of origin.

It is a best practice to cross integrate between metadata and data quality that brings out information like lineage, System of Origin (SoO), System of Record (SoR) etc. This information can be leveraged to explore further into the data value chain, and provide an analysis. But, to start leveraging this information from data dictionaries, it should be captured and chapter 4 provides more details of a meta-model that is self-sufficient to aid Data Quality Exploration and Analysis.

Data Quality Validation Routines or Checks

Business operations would be only interested in having fit-for-purpose-data. They would not have a complete understanding on the type of data quality validations to be performed to get this data to be usable. The business data stewards from the division will bridge the understanding of the business operations in identifying the quality requirements and taking them forth to the technical stewards and data quality analysts.

There are multiple data quality dimensions that can be leveraged by the data quality analysts in identifying the type of quality validation to be performed. As showcased in Table 5.8, a dimension like completeness ensures "availability of required data in a column, field, object or group of columns". There can be further sub-dimensions like "*count of records*", "*frequency distribution*", "*fill rate*" that can be associated with sub-dimensions of completeness.

- A check like "*count of records*" ensures that there is no loss of data, if data is distributed from a lead generation system to a customer master database, on conversion of lead to a customer. This action is ensured by performing a checksum or a count of records between the transmitting and receiving systems.
- A check like "*fill rate*" ensures that if a KYC due diligence or enhanced due diligence is being performed on a customer, the fill rate of the customer name, address and beneficiary name should be 100% complete.
- A check like "*frequency distribution*" is more of a technique rather than a validation routine, which can be used to look at a distribution of values across a timeline. If there is a period, where the data values for a data element like time weighted rate of return, are not present, the impact can be analyzed. Or, if a table is analyzed for frequency distribution, the number of blank, null or constant values in a column or set of columns in a table can be presented.

Further, the chapter will explore how to select the right validation routine, which needs to be applied in during a particular phase of the POSMAD.

Dimensions	Description	Sub Dimension
Accuracy	Refers to the degree that the value represents a real life entities they model	
Completeness	Availability of required data attributes and records	Count of Records Frequency distribution Fill rate
Consistency	Ensuring values in one dataset are consistent with another	Record consistency Structural consistency Semantic Consistency Pattern Analysis
Currency	Degree to which information is current to be applied	
Precision	Level of details on the characteristics of data elements	
Reasonableness	Level of consistency in operational context	
Referential Integrity	Condition that exists when all intended references from data in one column of a table to data in another column of same or different table	
Timeliness	Expectation of availability of the data by specified interval	Manual Float System Float
Uniqueness	No entity exists more than once	Duplicacy Redundancy
Validity	Ensures data values confirm to numerous characteristics like range of values	Range of Values Decimals Content check

Table 5.8: Data Quality Dimensions

It is required to clearly identify the type of data quality checks that need to be performed in a specific scenario and for a particular data life-cycle stage. It makes sense to perform a consistency check if data is in motion between endpoints but not at rest. The validation routines are shown in Table 5.8 above.

Completeness

Subroutine: Count of Records

- **Description**: is a quantitative validation routine where availability of data in a column or a field is checked after transmission
- **Usage**: The type of check is run against systems distributing and receiving data.
- **Validity Condition**: Target record count should match with the source record count.

Exhibit 5.6: Count of Records

Subroutine: Column Count

- **Description:** is a quantitative validation routine, where availability of data in a column or a field is checked for completeness
- **Usage**: The type of check is run against columns, tables where 100% of values or a specific percentage of values are required to fulfill a business scenario

- **Validity Condition**: 100% of the values in a column should be available.

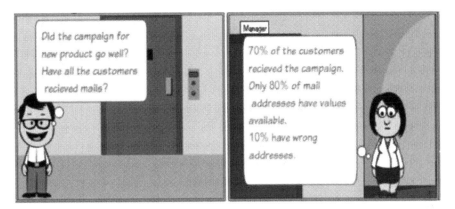

Exhibit 5.7: Column count

Validity

Subroutine: Validity

- **Description**: is a quantitative validation routine where 100% valid, unique and distinct values are checked in a column.
- **Usage**: The type of check should be run against any data when non-usable values need to be removed
- **Validity Condition**: 100% of the values in a column should be available

107

Exhibit 5.8: Validity

Subroutine: Range of Values

- **Description**: is a quantitative validation routine where values need to be in a specific range of Minimum and Maximum values
- **Usage**: The type of check can be run against any master data, transactional data
- **Validity Condition: 100% of the values should conform to a range**

Exhibit 5.9: Range of Values

Timeliness

Subroutine: Currency

- **Description**: is a quantitative validation routine that describes how updated is the data in the column for usage.
- **Usage**: The type of check should be run against any data where it needs to be current
- **Validity Condition:** The last change date should be in the valid range that as can be used in the Business scenario

Exhibit 5.10: Timeliness

Sub Routine: Information Lag

- **Description**: is a quantitative validation routine that describes the time lag between the real-world object changes and when the data represents the changes
- **Usage:** The type of check should be run against any data to check if data is not available in the receiving system by the time needed.
- **Validity Condition**: The data should be available in the receiving

system, process by the time it is intended to for processing of a use case

Exhibit 5.11: Information lag

Consistency

Subroutine: Row Level Consistency

- **Description**: is a quantitative validation routine that is used to check if related fields in the same record are consistent
- **Usage**: The type of check should be run against any data where relevance and meaning are provided when related fields are checked like the zip code matching with the address.
- **Validity Condition**: There should be 100% consistency in the related records in a row or multiple rows

Exhibit 5.12.1: Row Level Consistency

Exhibit 5.12.2: Row Level Consistency

Subroutine: Semantic Consistency

- **Description**: is a quantitative validation routine that is used to check if the a business term that exists physically across different datastores, holds the same meaning and context
- **Usage**: The type of check should be run against any data where relevance and meaning of the business term should be the same irrespective of where it occurs and is applied.
- **Validity Condition**: There should be 100% consistency in the related records across various data stores.

Exhibit 5.13: Semantic Consistency

The scope of data quality assessment can include identifying any issue that prevents data from being applied and producing the desired outcome. The profiling results from the assessment provide a platform to explore and analyze data quality using the dimensions stated in section "**Data Quality Validation Routines or Checks**". The issues related to all data quality dimensions will be validated, prioritized and recovered through the remediation cycle with the involvement of data owner and guidance from data steward. Issues related to integration between systems will be fixed by ensuring consistency in the data values across systems through business rules, transformation, derivation and consistency rules.

Data Quality Remediation

A data quality remediation solution can be termed as a service domain. As a starting point, the capabilities should range from having to identify, to documenting data quality issues. Next, comes the process of assigning them to the data owner or system SMEs, which require workflow capabilities. Further, the capabilities of collaborating, analyzing, performing root cause analysis (RCA), documenting business impact as well as reporting and closure should be available to remediate data quality issues. There are many tools in the market that have these capabilities and can be further customized based on the operating model and organization structure. Throwing in some scorecard and dashboard capabilities will help in reporting.

Where there is an implementation of master and reference data management solutions, the third-party data and internal data will be leveraged to automatically correct data to its accuracy while also certifying the golden record.

It is necessary to put in policies and procedures for manual data cleansing and remediation, procedures and guidelines along with integrating other data management services, such as metadata as well as governance.

Analysis of Reference Data Quality

- Reference data values are a slowly changing dimension and do not require the same kind of data quality monitoring once they are standardized. How often does a new country get added to the list of country codes or new products get added to the existing list? The metadata model can be leveraged to capture the current and future reference data standards. This would include the data element name including the capture of allowable values and, the name of the standard along with other required metadata. The existing solution for reference data can be leveraged or a new schema can be built to store reference data while a front end is provided for self-service capabilities in order to show reference data standards and values. The data ownership and stewardship processes will cater to the governance of reference data while specific reference data management process will cater to the management of the values and labels. Reference data will be classified into

- Global reference data standard across the group
- Local reference data standard in a business unit, system or process

Promotion from local to global reference data standards will follow the proposal, vetting and endorsement process. This will be a Governance process and can be initiated by the data owner or data steward or a cross-functional stewardship committee. With a goal of rationalizing reference data across the organization, reference data standards should be enforced on all business terms. Based on the criticality of the business term, they can be prioritized for rationalization.

Differentiating Data Quality Assessment from Monitoring

Today, the chief data offices have put in data quality processes that have the minimum activities, such as profiling based on need and remediation based on impact. But, the data quality process encompasses a larger process than the activities just quoted above. The processes of having to assess data quality come as a first step. To assess data quality, either the data should have been in error or should have been identified as a critical. It is necessary to understand the characteristics of the data, such as type, length, requirements for nullability, and minimum and maximum values that can come out of the data profiling. On pulling characteristics of data, such as an age, where the range can be between 10 to 120, the policy can be checked to see what the age is for having to invest into a certain product with the bank. If the same data element age needs to be used in `the context of a specific product, the data owner and steward can come up with a specialized or contextualized data quality requirement that states the age should range between 30-60 for a retirement finance product. This is the outcome of having to come up with data quality assessment that ends by having data rules documented. Further, the rules can be promoted to the group, in case they are common across, while any localized rules can be associated with the domain alone.

Now, starts the need for data quality monitoring, where the data tends to change frequently. If this changing data is prone to errors, the same can be monitored continuously through a rules run. However, all the data rules need not be run continuously, and it is only required to run only the data quality rules, such as completeness or integrity, which pull out the data quality issues as they appear. One rule of thumb is to have the data sampled and profiled based on the frequency it is refreshed, to sense the occurrence of data quality issues associated with specific validations.

Summary

Actively maintaining accurate, valid and consistent data is essential to provide excellence in regular business operations. The new normal is not just having fit-for-purpose data but to actively assess and monitor data-at-rest and data-in-motion, as well. Today in enterprises, most data quality activities are performed in silos, across the organization's divisions and systems. Perhaps, the trust in using that data lies with the business unit alone but not with another business unit that sources the same data. Thus, comes the need to standardize and centralize these activities into services that builds transparency and trust into the data across the organization. On go-live of these data quality service operations, there will be consistent outcomes across divisions receiving promotions on the benefits of assessing and monitoring data quality.

6

POLICY OR GUIDELINES TO FORMALIZE DATA MANAGEMENT?

If current policies are not sufficient to meet the business needs, there is a necessity to identify the changes necessary to implement the desired future state. The policy can be enforced through the business rules in processes or workflow. Guidelines can guide the behavior of the personnel and is not a compulsion, as they are embedded in procedures. Organizations create data policy to ensure enforcement of compliance with mandatory regulatory, internal compliance, best practices, and legal and ethical requirements along with the need for managing risk. These requirements are embedded into the policy and privacy statements to provide guidance to personnel on their accountabilities and responsibilities. This assists the personnel in carrying out any activity that includes data-related operations. This helps manage the risks in data processes, thus aligning with risk appetite and tolerance levels. The organizations have to decide to drive governance with either guidelines or policy as is the similar dilemma today in most organizations to enable decisions through a governance committee or a limited membership council. The organization's enabling culture should assist the governance function in taking the foundationals calls to drive by poicy or guidelines.

A sample data sourcing policy has been presented below that clearly articulates the summary of the policy, what is an outcome of this policy, and the responsibilities, and accountabilities of various roles in sourcing data.

Policy Summary:

- Data must be made available based on the enterprise needs to process, people and applications
- There must be only one primary source of each data element
- Data must be sourced in agreement with the data transfer protocols, and country-specific policies
- Data that is derived or transformed must be documented from the sources, both internal and external

Guidelines

- There must be an authoritative source system of record or golden source identified for all critical data
- A data element should have a golden copy or a system of reference, which is to be a read-only source
- Data should be sourced only from a certified system of record or a system of reference
- The data consumer should get into an agreement with the data provider and mention any transfer agreements as per data movement policy and/or any quality requirements as per data quality policy

System of Record or Golden Source

- Is the data storage system that is considered an authoritative source of a data element
- It can be external to the enterprise

- Other copies should be considered secondary but must replicate the data within Service Level Agreement (SLA) as per the agreement, to ensure timeliness and currency
- Data that is enhanced or transformed outside the golden source will the responsibility of the stakeholders or application, performing the transformation

Calculated data

- Golden copies or systems of reference should not be the System o record for any data created by complex calculation
- A simple calculation can include addition, subtraction, multiplication, a division of 2 or 3 variables.
- Complex calculations include more than three variables. For example, calculation of risk exposure for Basel-II

Data Management Office

- Accountable to ensure that metadata repository is populated with systems of record or golden sources as well as golden copies or systems of reference
- Responsible for ensuring the Key Performance Indicators (KPIs) for the workflow to certify the golden sources and golden copies
- Responsible for standardizing framework and, workflow to manage the attributes related to golden sources and golden copies
- Accountable for submitting reports to the council and board on the data availability in golden sources and copies

Data Owner

- Accountable to accept proposals, certify a data store as golden source or golden copy for critical data elements
- Responsible for providing data dictionaries with the information of golden sources or copies
- Accountable for determining a change to the designation of golden source or golden copy by initiating the workflow
- Responsible for triggering the generation of the profile for a data element from a data store

Data Steward

- Responsible for determining a change to the designation of golden source or golden copy by initiating the workflow
- Responsible for proposing data store as golden source or golden copy for critical data elements
- Responsible for ensuring that data owners are certifying data stores
- Accountable to liaise with business data stewards from other units to understand the wanted and the unwanted redundancy in the data, that is shared with the data owner
- Accountable for continuous elicitation of feedback on golden sources and to, copy the standardization process
- Accountable to ensure the certification is complete on time within SLA

Project, Program Group

- Responsible for notifying the governance representative if the solution capabilities include acquiring, creating, storing, sharing, integration, and distributing data from data source not certified as golden sources or copies.

- For data that does not have a designated golden source or copy, responsible for coordinating with the data owner to identify the proposed golden source or copy

Thus a policy or guideline should clearly state all the aspects of:
- Purpose of the policy
- Criticality or categorization
- Boundaries of scope
- Outcomes
- Who will addressed by the policy
- Role of stakeholders/Function
- Responsible and Accountable for which aspects
- Balance of responsibility and Accountability
- Processes, workflows or links to procedures that provide guidance to personnel
- SLA and escalation mechanism
- Requirement for creation of additional groups (associated charters) for cross-functional forums
- Related policies or procedures
- Audit frequency
- Review mechanism

Whether an organization decides to drive governance and management by policy or guidelines is a call to be made by the executive ownership in conjunction with the leadership. I have seen organizations that were high in maturity and were using guidelines, while I have also seen organizations that use policy but may not be adhering or enforcing it through required programs.

Summary

In summary, guidelines are considered to have a positive impact on the personnel and their belief systems. While the firm is not enforcing a personnel to carry out a specific task in a particular way, it is necessary to understand that whenever there is a decision to be taken such as sourcing data, guidelines pave the way to achieve a consistent outcome. Policy on the other hand is an enforcement, on the organizational activities. An organization that is policy heavy, gets to pile on new governance policies to it's existing list. There might be a need for self-assessment or audit on how well the data management and governance policy is orchestrated. This can change gradually as the organizations get to embrace a data driven culture actively.

7

ASSESSING VALUE FROM DATA MANAGEMENT AND GOVERNANCE

Every data governance service and activity will be considered as governance enabler. An enabler, in a simple sense, is a new or an improved capability made available by data management and governance division. These enablers can be further classified into business, process and technology enablers.

- *"Policymaking"* is a business enabler
- *"Metadata service management"* is a process enabler
- *"Data profiling"* is a technology enabler

Every governance enabler should have a metric associated with a measurement like person hours spent on metadata management or the number of business terms included in the glossary. The data stewards then, within each division, should get to document and publish divisional business and data value chains.

Metrics and Ownership

The stewards along with divisions discover the success factors and metrics used to measure the commercial success of the division like time to service, customer service effectiveness, cross-sell ratio and much more. Then, a trace is established between governance enablers and the divisional value chains. Get the divisions to agree and own the metrics. This is what creates dialogue and awareness in the divisions where governance needs to step in. The value realization framework should clearly outlay the traceability between *governance enablers – > technology and process impact – > business impact and value as shown in Exhibit 7.1*

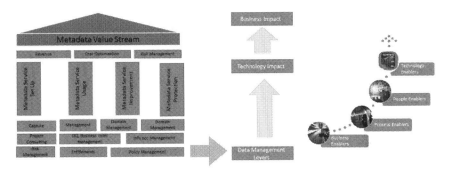

Exhibit 7.1: Metadata value realization model

Sample Scenarios

For example, Metadata capture and data mapping activities as enablers

1. Lead to reduction in person hours spent on performing data analysis

2. Further, reduces the requirements turnaround time

3. Finally, puts you in a competitive position in the market with product or Service time to market.

The lack of focus is common in data governance divisions across industries and is constantly affecting how people think of data governance activities. There are immediate and cumulative benefits from having to manage metadata or data quality. But, you need a benefits management and assessment framework to realize the benefits from these services.

Some data governance divisions kickstart their initiatives with insightful business cases that rightly overcome organizational challenges. These business cases should clearly articulate tangible benefits of using the data management services. In other organizations, the data management services are implemented as a big bang across all divisions. In this case, benefits would be monitored and measured on a continuous basis in accordance with an assessment plan. Most organizations are not orchestrating governance activities as initiatives but rather as a continuous push or pull based services. It is strongly recommended that one has a performance assessment plan before starting a data governance service be it data quality or metadata management. This plan should bring out the approach to monitor and measure the value of orchestration over specific timelines.

Quoting the second example, what does a 10% increase in the accuracy of the leads dataset mean to your marketing division and organization?

1. It directly impacts the ROI.

2. The division efficiently utilizes the budget allocated to the campaign and embraces a high conversion rate that leads to the revenue increase.

And a third example as well: what does de-duplication of the customer primary accounts mean to the organization?

1. The service executive on a call spends less time on a call with a customer to get to the right customer account by not having to struggle with duplicate accounts.

2. This directly impacts your customer satisfaction score and, cross-sell ratio while also reducing operating costs with maintaining duplicate accounts and time spent in getting the right account.

Summary

It is equally important to show progress in activey managing data and having a quantifiable measure against use of enabling activities, outcomes and benefits. A benefits realization model should be owned by the business units or divisions leveraging the data management services as the benefits of managing and governing data is embraced by these divisions. The stewards will help leverage the levers of data management services, while they also help the division in defining and owning the metrics and the impact that the levers have on the success factors of the division. The need of the hour is to have a right model that has a judicious mix of qualitative and quantitative benefits that can be used for assessment and monitoring the data management and governance services. This further will support the sustainability of data management and governance in the organization.

Closing Word

Organizations are enabling growth through new and pervasive technology capabilities like big data analytics, machine learning, Internet of Things (IOT) and semantics. While data is being considered by most organizations as an Enterprise asset, some organizations are actively managing and governing this life plasma that is also increasing the trust amongst diverse stakeholders. Standardizing the data management and governance activities into definitive services with clear boundaries, increases consistency in usage, outcomes and benefits. This book provides step by step simple and effective approaches to setup and ope-rationalize data management services that will realize the benefits of leveraging valid, accurate and meaningful data. A target state control environment embraced throughout the book should help simplify the data landscape and manage data as a crowd sourced meaning that reduces the total costs and enables growth through data capabilities.

Made in the USA
Columbia, SC
15 June 2022

61764367R00076